MONIC J. AYOTTE, RP

The B.E.C.O.M.I.N.G Method

Life...

BEYOND LIMITING BELIEFS

The B.E.C.O.M.I.N.G. Method
Life... Beyond Limiting Beliefs

Art Direction including Book Cover, Typesetting, and Layout Design by LeadHer Publishing

Cover Design - Christina Williams, LeadHer Publishing

Editing - Kim Collins

Interior Design - Christina Williams, LeadHer Publishing

ISBN Print - 978-1-998411-40-5

ISBN Ebook - 978-1-998411-41-2

For more information on the author, visit www.becomingnow.ca, Monic Ayotte on Facebook or @becomingnow on social channels.

For more information on the publisher, visit leadherpublishing.com or @leadherpublishing on social channels.

DEDICATION

To my Warrior Mom…

My biggest fan,

my greatest teacher,

and the love of my life.

Disclaimer

This book is intended for educational and informational purposes only. It is not a substitute for psychotherapy, psychological counseling, medical advice, diagnosis, or treatment.

Every individual's situation is unique. Readers experiencing mental health concerns or emotional distress are encouraged to seek support from a qualified and licensed healthcare professional.

Reading this book does not establish a therapist–client relationship..

AUTHOR'S NOTE

The concepts, tools, and therapeutic frameworks explored in this book are drawn from decades of research, clinical application, and real-life transformation. I honor and acknowledge the work of all the researchers, scientists, and healers whose wisdom laid the foundation for this work. This book offers my personal integration, interpretation, and application of these teachings—crafted into a unified system of healing and transformation that I call the **B.E.C.O.M.I.N.G. Method**.

Foreword

Every so often, you meet someone whose courage to face their truth cracks something open in everyone around them, giving them permission to do the same. Monic is one of those people. What I admire most about her is that she never pretends the inner work is easy. She has battled an eating disorder, endured the ache of never feeling good enough, and carried the relentless weight of her own inner critic. She has lived with fear, shame, and self-doubt long enough to know their voices by heart. She has confronted the stories she's carried from childhood. And instead of hiding her pain, or running from it, she chose to meet it head-on and to transform it into something that could help others heal. Over the years, I've had the privilege of mentoring Monic at different points along her journey, and I've witnessed the courage it took for her to challenge the beliefs that once kept her scared, stuck, and small. I remember one particular conversation we had when she was torn between staying on a secure career path or following her dream of going back to school to complete her master's degree and become a psychotherapist. On the surface, staying in teaching made perfect sense: good pay, great benefits, and the kind of stability most people dream about. But for Monic, it didn't fit. Her soul was calling for something different — something truer to her deeper purpose in life. Walking away, though, meant starting over. It meant trading certainty for risk, a steady paycheck for student loans, and the comfort of knowing exactly what the next twenty years would hold for the unknown of building a new life from the ground up. It also meant letting go of an identity she had built, and the safety of being seen as "successful" — for the risk of being judged as never satisfied, as unrealistic for chasing a new dream at her age, or even as reckless for walking away from a life most people would never dare give up. Stepping away felt terrifying. But the thought of staying and shrinking into a life that wasn't truly her own was even more unbearable. What struck me in that moment was that even under the weight of so many fears — of failure, of being criticized, of not being enough or being too much, there was a quiet determination. Monic didn't want to keep walking a path that kept her small, both physically and psychologically. She longed for a life that was truly her own. Watching her choose courage in that first step, and then continue to choose her truth again and again, is what makes her path, and this book, so powerful. Because this choice wasn't simply a brave career move; it was a reflection of her healing. It was a decision to stop letting fear, shame, or anyone else's expectations dictate her life. What you'll find in this book isn't just theory, it's lived experience. It's Monic's willingness to be vulnerable, and her ability to turn her struggles into wisdom and practical tools you can use in your own life. As you read, you'll see her humanity, her resilience, and her honesty. You'll be invited to face your own truth, challenge the patterns that have kept you stuck, and imagine a life where fear, shame, and doubt no longer lead the way, and where other people's opinions no longer have the final say. This book will remind you that you are not broken, and that what once protected you may now be preventing you from living the life of your dreams. And if you let it, these pages will shine a light into the hidden places where old patterns, self-doubt, and limiting beliefs have kept you small. They will remind you that you're not alone. And most importantly, they will remind you that you too have a choice — to stop shrinking into who you were told to be, and to start fully stepping into who you authentically are.

With admiration and gratitude,

Lise Leblanc

Therapist, Author, YouTube Creator

Preface

I once read that nearly 80% of people dream of writing a book, yet only 3% ever finish, and less than 0.5% go on to publish. For most of my life, I belonged to the 80% group. I carried the dream quietly, secretly, always brushing up against it but never fully reaching for it. Not because I lacked ideas, passion, or purpose, but because I believed something unspoken yet deeply embedded: that people like me could dream big… but not achieve big.

That belief ran like a current beneath so many of my choices. Until one day, I paused and asked a simple, powerful question: *Says who?* Who decided that this dream wasn't for me? Who said I wasn't enough? I started tracing the roots of those lies, the subtle, insidious stories that had shaped how I saw myself and what I thought I was capable of. And as I did, I saw how those invisible threads were still weaving themselves into every corner of my life.

This book was born out of the moment I woke up to that hard truth: I was still, after decades of healing, living under rules I never agreed to, inside a story that was never truly mine.

That reckoning? It changed everything.

More than words on a page, this book is a mirror, a companion, and a powerful tool for anyone ready to do the same. It's for the dreamers, the seekers, the ones who've always known there was more.

And for you to truly understand the power it holds, I felt you needed to know where it came from. Because it wasn't written from theory. It was written from experience, from decades of walking the winding path of healing, rising, and BECOMING. It came from me learning to believe in what's possible again.

So here goes...

In my work as a psychotherapist and hypnotist, I've come to recognize a truth that reveals itself again and again: people aren't just seeking relief from pain, they're reaching for something deeper. Beneath the exhaustion, the anxiety, and the patterns they no longer want to repeat, there's often a quiet but persistent whisper: *There has to be more to life than this.*

They don't come looking for quick fixes. They come searching for transformation, not just to mend what feels broken, but to reclaim something essential, to remember who they are, and to create lives rooted in meaning, power, and purpose. And what I've witnessed time and time again is nothing short of awe-inspiring: courage rising through fear, clarity cutting through confusion, and the unwavering drive to become who they were always meant to be, even in the wake of trauma, grief, and addiction.

This book is for them. And it's for you.

If you've ever felt that whisper stirring inside you, the one that speaks in quiet moments and shows up when things feel off. If you've felt the pull toward something more, something truer, then hear this: you're not broken. You're being called. And you're exactly where you're meant to be.

I've felt it too. I've stood in that sacred in-between, between who I was and who I could become. And even after decades of healing, I found myself face-to-face with long-buried beliefs still quietly shaping my life. I had done the work. I thought I was free. But truth has a way of resurfacing when you're ready to rise.

At first, I ignored it. I dismissed the ache and pushed away the discomfort. But transformation doesn't wait for convenience. It doesn't show up when the timing is perfect. It arrives like a disruption, a sacred invitation. And it will keep showing up until you listen.

For me it came like a storm, shattering the old stories I had outgrown, the ones that told me to shrink, to stay small, to settle. And in that shattering, I heard it clearly: *This is your time.* If you're feeling that same tug, the stirring, the restlessness, the sense that you're meant for more, trust it. It's not your undoing. It's your *becoming.* And your breakthrough starts here.

The Catalyst

For as long as I can remember, I've felt a pull to color outside the lines, to stretch, to rise, to rewrite the rules. Playing small never suited me. I've always been drawn to the edge, to boldness, and to the thrill of dreaming wildly and unapologetically.

But that fire? It wasn't born overnight.

It was forged slowly, through decades of inner work, healing, and the shedding of everything I was never meant to be. Layer by layer, I peeled back the false stories I had carried. I met my shadows. I honored my wounds. And in the process, I uncovered a truth too clear to ignore: **I was meant for more.**

It was not in an ego-driven way, but in a soul-deep, cellular knowing. What I once framed as "playing with the Big Dogs" became something else entirely, an intuitive, relentless call to rise and to step into the fullness of who I came here to be.

And rise I did. Or so I thought.

By spring of 2023, it looked like I was finally living fully in my truth: bold career moves, heart-led risks, and loud declarations of *"Go big or go home."* From the outside, it looked like courage, conviction, and expansion. And in many ways, it was. But behind the boldness, something quieter was still holding on: **fear.**

While one foot pushed forward into growth, the other stayed rooted in the safety of smallness. That was the part I hadn't admitted, not to anyone, not even to myself.

The truth? I still carried beliefs that told me to shrink, to stay agreeable, and to not take up too much space. I deeply believed in the message I was sharing with the world about limitless possibilities. But I hadn't yet fully turned that belief inward. I hadn't faced the subconscious whispers still echoing beneath my boldness:

What if you fail again? What if you're not enough?

I was living boldly, yes, but only up to the edge of my unhealed limiting beliefs. And that quiet conflict? That was my reckoning. I began to notice the invisible threads still woven through my life, threads spun from old programming, quiet fears, and a subtle belief that maybe now I was "just enough." I wasn't resisting growth. I simply hadn't realized how much I was still operating from stories that weren't mine. That was the humbling part. The woman guiding others to step into their power... was still hesitating to fully claim her own. The irony wasn't lost on me. And neither was the invitation.

Once again, I found myself in quiet awe of the subconscious mind, its patterns, its whispers, its fierce devotion to keeping me safe. And once again, I welcomed the lesson. And the moment I stopped pretending I was already "all in"... the moment I allowed myself to see where I was still playing small, still shrinking, still hiding beneath the armor of *almost*, that's when the real transformation began.

What I've learned is that stepping into your power isn't one grand, fearless moment. It's a collection of small, sacred decisions to rise, softly, bravely, imperfectly, every time life invites you to.

2023—The Invitation

The year began as my most expansive yet, professionally, financially, and spiritually. I had stepped fully into my role as a healer. My psychotherapy and hypnosis practice was thriving, my clients were transforming, and I felt deeply aligned with my purpose. Every sign pointed to more growth, more possibility, and more impact.

I was building something beautiful. I had big visions, a collaborative wellness center, innovative mindfulness-based programs, and a life that reflected everything I'd worked so hard to create.

And then, in April, the phone rang. *Cancer.* Aggressive. My mother.

Time stopped. The ground beneath me shifted. In a single moment, everything I had built, everything I had dreamed of, quietly faded into the background. Without hesitation, I stepped into the role of caregiver, not out of guilt, not out of obligation, but out of love, a deep, aching, fierce kind of love. Or at least, that's what I told myself.

My dreams could wait. They had to wait.

I didn't ease into caregiving. I threw myself into it, fully, completely, and without question. Somewhere deep down, I believed that I had to be extraordinary, an even better daughter, a stronger sister, a more selfless caregiver. Somehow, who I was didn't feel like enough anymore. So I became the good daughter. The dependable one. The one who could handle it all. I wore that identity like armor, never realizing it was built from a quiet, aching need to prove my worth.

Somewhere beneath the care and the selflessness, I was still chasing something: The hope that if I just gave enough, if I just held it all together, I could keep everything and everyone okay.

But the unraveling had begun, quietly, slowly, and unseen. With every sleepless night, every hospital visit and chemo treatment, I was pulled deeper into the grip of fear. I couldn't hear my intuition anymore. The voice that once guided me with clarity had gone silent beneath the noise of panic and self-imposed responsibility. And the whispers in my mind? They turned cruel.

- *"There's no room for your dreams right now."*
- *"This isn't about you."*
- *"Be small. Be quiet. Be good."*

And I listened. I believed them.

Then came November. My mom fell. A broken hip. Surgery. Hospital stays. Medication induced deliriums.

I watched my mother, the woman who raised me with strength and determined optimism, slip into confusion and pain. While her body was fighting cancer and healing a fracture, her mind was fighting to hold on to herself. And I... I was fighting to hold it all together.

But the truth? I was terrified. Terrified of losing her, of losing the connection that had grounded me my whole life. My biggest fan. My anchor. I watched her suffer, and I couldn't stop it. The helplessness was suffocating. I would have given anything, *anything*, to trade places, to take away her pain and her fears, to protect her from what none of us could control. I was desperate. And when desperation takes the wheel, love can turn frantic. I overstepped with family members. I clung too tightly. I tried to control the uncontrollable. And in that chaos, words spilled out that I would give anything to take back. Words, not born out of malice but coming from a place so full of fear and grief it spilled over into every conversation.

And then came the feedback, the words I received as criticism, delivered by the people I loved most. Each one landed like a blade, not just wounding but revealing. They cut straight to the heart of a belief I hadn't even realized still lived inside me:

I'm not enough.

It echoed through every cell of my body, that old, familiar ache I had carried for as long as I could remember, a quiet wound shaped by years of conditioning, whispering that love had to be earned, that worth was conditional, and that my place, whether in my family, in the world, or in someone's heart, depended on being *good enough*, selfless *enough*, and perfect *enough*. I had spent my life chasing that elusive "enough," and still, it never felt within reach.

That wound had been waiting patiently in the shadows. And now, it didn't whisper. It roared. I unraveled. Not with a bang, but with a slow, silent collapse. I kept showing up for everyone, but I was pouring from an empty cup. I was hollow. My grief wasn't just about what was happening with my mom. I was mourning the woman I used to be, the version of me who felt strong, grateful, and like a true visionary. I missed her. I didn't know how to find her again.

And still, the world kept asking for more. And I kept giving. I had trained everyone to expect it, to see me as the strong one. But inside, I was in pieces. The weight was unbearable. The exhaustion, bone-deep. And beneath it all, the deepest ache of all: the looming, unspoken truth that I might lose my mother, that one day I would wake up, and she would be gone. And I didn't know how to live in a world without her.

Her pain, her fear, her fight… it became my everything. And the love I felt for her… it brought me to my knees. Because when you love someone that much, the thought of losing them is not just heartbreaking, it's shattering.

To the friends who checked in, held space, and showed up in ways that reminded me love has many forms, even in the comfort of a hearty plate of Chicken Parmigiana - thank you. Your presence meant more than words could ever say.

And to ***my person***, the one who saw past the brave face, who stood steady through every storm, who held me not to heal me but to honor what was breaking, there are no words big enough. You were my calm in the chaos, my reminder that I was never truly alone. My gratitude for you lives deep in my bones.

2023 unraveled me in ways I never saw coming. It stripped away my certainty and shattered the illusion that I had it all together. It humbled me, not with cruelty but with precision. It pushed me to the edge of what I thought I could handle and then showed me the places within that still ached for attention, tenderness, and truth. In the undoing, it gave me something unexpected: an invitation back to my own life. It made me soft again, honest again, and whole in ways I didn't know I was fractured.

2023 taught me more than any year before it. It challenged my limits. But it also gave me a gift I never expected. It revealed the places that still needed healing, and in doing so, it made space for something greater. It made me human again. The events of 2023 dismantled the version of me I thought I had to be, and in the aftermath, I found the space to ***become*** who I am meant to be.

The turning point came quietly.

I woke one morning in early 2024 feeling this incredible sadness, resentment, and overall sense of dread. My body, once my place of refuge, felt tight and restless. My chest buzzed with anxiety. The calm, grounded state I had come to know as my baseline, my home frequency, was nowhere to be found. In its place: fear, stress, and a deep sense of disconnection. And then came the whisper, not from my mind, but from somewhere deeper.

How did I get here?

It stopped me in my tracks. Because I knew I had drifted. Slowly. Subtly. Silently. Away from myself. Away from the peace I had worked so hard to cultivate. That question was quickly followed by another:

How do I get back?

That moment became my reckoning, not in a dramatic, life-flashing-before-my-eyes kind of way, but in a quiet, soul-level knowing that I couldn't keep going like this. I wasn't well. I wasn't happy. And I certainly wasn't at peace. So I did the only thing I knew to do: I returned to the work. Because I knew from decades of walking this beautiful path to wellness that if I wanted to move forward, I had to find my way back to myself, to my center, to what was real.

The Transformation

As I write these words in 2025, there's a stillness in me now, a peace that for a time felt impossible. The chaos, the heartbreak, and the unraveling of 2023 no longer sits like a weight on my chest. It lives inside me as wisdom, as strength, as proof that even in the darkest moments, something beautiful can be born.

What once felt like the end was, in truth, my ***becoming***. But how did I get here? How did I go from breaking down to breaking through? I stopped hiding from myself, from the truth, from the patterns that kept me small. I faced it all. The fear. The guilt. The blaming. The stories I had inherited and repeated for far too long. And then, I made a choice, a powerful, soul-level decision: *I will no longer abandon myself.*

That decision changed everything. Because the moment you choose healing, truly choose it, life rushes in to meet you. The right people show up. The right wisdom arrives. The universe opens a door. And when it did, I walked through, tender, humbled, and ready. I surrendered to the lessons. I leaned into the pain. I listened to the whispers of my soul and to the stillness between the noise. I stopped trying to control and started learning to trust. I let the grief move through me, in its own time, in its own way, and in doing so, it also set me free.

Years of inner work, quiet devotion, and showing up for myself over and over again prepared me for this moment. And when it came, I didn't run. I rose. I began again. This time not from urgency, but from truth. I meditated with purpose. I moved with intention. I let gratitude flood me, not just for the light, but for the darkness that shaped me. The fear, the grief, the unraveling, they didn't break me. They molded me, refined me, and brought me home to myself.

Today, I no longer define myself by what I've experienced. I see a woman who is grounded, radiant, wildly human, and deeply, unapologetically alive and driven. I love her, not because she's perfect but because she rose. And because she keeps rising.

This is what transformation looks like.

It's messy. It's magnificent. It's layer after layer of unbecoming what never belonged and stepping into what's always been true. It's not linear. It's not always easy. But it is beautiful and *always* worth it. And more than anything, it's a choice. It's a choice to show up, again and again. To meet yourself with compassion. To rewrite the story. To rise and *become*. Every single day, I choose:

To meet myself in love.

To challenge limiting stories.

To break old patterns and breathe in new truths.

To live with gratitude, for *all* of it.

To stand tall in my bigness, my brilliance, my *becoming*.

To speak boldly, ask boldly, receive boldly.

To trust my intuition and let it lead the way.

To choose presence over perfection.

To choose love, always.

And because I choose, I no longer wait. I create. I claim. I *am*.

Now, I turn to you. Are you ready to let go of the stories that have kept you small? Are you ready to ***become,*** to step into a life that feels aligned, authentic, and alive?

If you've been waiting for a sign, this is it. All you have to do… is say yes.

Well then, let's do this!

Introduction

B.E.C.O.M.I.N.G.

This is your invitation. Not a polite one. A powerful one. A soul-stirring, heart-igniting, *life-changing* invitation to break free from the limiting beliefs that have kept you stuck and standing in the way of the life you were always meant to live.

It's your time.

It's time to stop playing small. It's time to stop just getting by. It's time to stop waiting for the perfect moment, the right sign, or someone else's permission to live the life that's been burning in your heart. This is your moment to rise. To expand. To *become.*

Together, we're going to get honest about the stories you've been telling yourself, the stories about who you are, what you're worth, and what you think you're allowed to have. Some of those stories were born out of survival, and yes, they once kept you safe. But now? They are keeping you stuck. They're keeping you from the joy, freedom, and power that are already yours. And we're not doing that anymore.

We'll dive into the incredible, untapped brilliance of your brain and reach into its power to change, evolve, and rewire. But this book isn't just about science. It's about your spirit. It's about your desire to feel whole, to be seen, to stop performing and start *becoming.* And here's what I need you to know, right from the start:

You are not broken.
You are not too late.

You are not too much or not enough.
You are *becoming.*

And everything you need, every ounce of strength, wisdom, courage, and clarity, is already inside you, waiting to be remembered.

So take a breath. Right here. Right now. Let this be your turning point.

You didn't land on this page by accident. That whisper inside you, the one that says *"there's more for me than this,"* is not your imagination. It's your ***becoming.*** It's your soul rising up to remind you that you were made for more.

But first, let's name the resistance. Step one is to confront and challenge the belief your mind may already be feeding you, the one whispering (or perhaps shouting) that this book is just another self-help guide, another title on the shelf destined to gather dust like so many before it. *That* belief is your first obstacle. It's the voice of doubt, of resistance, and of the part of you that fears hoping again because hope carries the risk of disappointment.

Recognize that voice for what it truly is: a defense mechanism built to protect you from hurt but is unintentionally holding you back from growth. It doesn't reflect the potential of this book or your ability to change; it's simply your mind clinging to what's familiar, even if that familiarity no longer serves you.

But here's the gift: the moment you recognize it... the moment you question it... the moment you *choose* to believe something different... that's when everything begins to change.

That's when the *becoming* begins. It begins the moment you stop buying into the belief that no longer serves you. By naming and challenging this belief, you're already stepping onto the path of rewiring your mind, rewriting your story, and opening the door to genuine possibility.

This book? It is your tool, your guide, and your opportunity to step into the life you've always intuitively known you're capable of living. It's not about quick fixes or empty promises. It's about real, lasting transformation. But here's the thing: it won't work unless *you* work.

You have to show up for yourself, face the doubts head on, and take that first brave step toward change.

Something within you is waking up, ready to break free from the old patterns, the old pain, the old roles you've outgrown. Let's follow that whisper together and see where it leads. I know that whisper well. It's lived inside me for years, guiding me into places I didn't always understand but always needed. That whisper is the voice of your becoming. It finds you when you're ready, even if you don't feel ready. And it will never give up on you, even when you've given up on yourself.

So trust it. Trust yourself. Let's follow it together.

You need to know that this journey isn't about perfection. It's not about fixing yourself. It's about *reclaiming* yourself. It's about becoming who you've always been beneath the fear, the shame, the conditioning, and the lies.

We'll uncover the hidden beliefs that have kept you playing small, and together, we'll break them wide open. We'll rewrite the narrative. We'll ignite your vision. We'll walk with power, purpose, and intention.

And we will do it with fire in our bellies and truth in our bones. Because becoming isn't something that happens to you. It's something you *choose.* And you've already chosen, by picking up this book, by being here, by listening to that inner whisper that refuses to be silenced any longer.

So let's begin. Let's burn the old stories down. Let's rise from the ashes. Let's ***become.***

The Formula

Let me be clear: the concepts in this book aren't uniquely mine. I didn't invent transformation. I have no problem with giving credit to the brilliant minds and the gurus that have blazed the wellness path for all of us. What is uniquely mine, what is deeply, fiercely *me*, is how I've lived it, how I've shaped, refined, and embodied these teachings into a cohesive, soul-aligned, practical formula that actually *works.*

This book is more than words on a page. It's a lifeline. It's a labor of love born from decades of lived experience, deep healing, and the sacred privilege of walking alongside others on their path to wholeness. It's a guide for breaking free from anxiety, addiction, burnout, old patterns, toxic relationships, and the inner narratives that have kept you from the life you know you're meant to live.

Within these pages, I share the 8-step formula that has not only changed my life but has transformed the lives of countless others. This isn't a theory. It's a proven process I call the B.E.C.O.M.I.N.G. Method, a framework that blends practical psychology, neuroscience, soulful self-inquiry, and embodied action. With it, you'll learn how to break the cycle of self-sabotage, take back control of your thoughts, and intentionally *become* who you were always meant to be.

At every step, you'll find reflective prompts, guided exercises, and tools that will help you move from confusion to clarity, from powerlessness to purpose, from hiding… to *becoming.*

Why do I believe so deeply in this formula? Because it saved me. Because it's been my lifeline, too. I've built this model brick by brick through decades of personal experience, through the raw, often painful journey of recovering from disordered eating, untangling myself from the grip of anxiety and depression. It guided me out of toxic relationships that drained every ounce of my energy, leaving me feeling utterly depleted, exhausted, and unimportant.

I've walked this path. I've stumbled, fallen hard, and gotten back up more times than I can even remember. But with every misstep and every rise, I've uncovered profound truths about resilience, healing, and the limitless potential for transformation that lives within all of us. I've been mentored by brilliant minds. I've studied the best. But more than anything, I've lived the questions and earned the answers. And now I offer them to you, so you can rise faster, fall less, and return home to yourself sooner.

Today, I choose to walk this path not as an expert standing above but as a woman rising beside you, hand outstretched, saying, *"Let's do this together.*" This is my way of paying it forward, my way of saying, "*You don't have to do this alone.*"

This formula that brought me back to myself in 2024 continues to be my anchor again and again, and it will bring you back too, when life shakes you, when fear whispers, when you forget who you are. It's here for you, not just to inform but to *transform*. If you're in a place of pain or uncertainty, this is your invitation to shift, to rise, to *become*.

I am beyond excited for what's in store for you. The journey you're about to take will awaken parts of yourself you never thought possible. I'm here to tell you, with all my heart, that the life you've been dreaming of is closer than you think, and it begins with this step-by-step approach to breaking free from limiting beliefs.

It begins with a single decision: to believe there's more and then to act on that belief, step by step, one brave page at a time. Before we dive in and get to work, there's one more piece of guidance I need to share with you. Consider it a heads up to set you up for success!

This journey is *not about blame*. It's not about pointing fingers at the people or circumstances that contributed to the beliefs that may still hold you back. We're not here to label anyone as "at fault" or get stuck in the heavy fog of resentment. That approach, while tempting, will only keep you bound to the very limitations you're seeking to break free from.

Instead, this process is about liberation, about gaining clarity and insight into the hidden patterns that have shaped your thinking for years, for decades. These patterns didn't form overnight, nor did they arise out of nowhere. They were born from experiences, relationships, and moments that, over time, left an imprint on your heart and mind. Some of these moments were small and subtle, like seeds planted in the fertile soil of your childhood. Others were monumental, defining moments that carved deep grooves into the way you see yourself and the world.

But let me tell you this: no matter how deeply rooted those beliefs feel, they are not immovable. They are not permanent. The beauty of this work is that by following the thread of these beliefs, tracing them back to their origins, you gain the power to untangle them. You gain the power to rewrite the stories that have defined you, and in doing so, you reclaim your ability to shape your future.

When I first began my healing journey decades ago, breaking free of these programs felt insurmountable. It felt as though I was betraying the very identity I had spent years constructing, an identity I thought was necessary for love, connection, and survival. But deep down, I knew that remaining stuck in these programs came at a price I could no longer afford to pay. Staying there meant losing more of myself each day, and I wasn't willing to let that happen any longer.

Today, I feel an immense sense of gratitude for the wisdom and resilience that rose from my recent encounter with limiting beliefs. It became a powerful reminder of the inner strength that lives within me and of the transformative tools I've gathered, honed, and embodied over the years to create meaningful, lasting change. This experience highlighted how far I've come and the incredible growth I've achieved in my life. It also reaffirmed the effectiveness of the 8-step B.E.C.O.M.I.N.G. Method I rely on, an approach that not only helped me navigate the pain of old patterns but also guided me to a place of greater clarity, strength, and self-awareness in my daily life.

The events of 2023, if anything, have reminded me of one profound truth: life's toughest moments are truly gifts, opportunities to step into greatness, if we allow them to be. They challenge us to refine our skills, test our resolve, and deepen our commitment to ourselves. I can confidently declare that these moments have only strengthened my dedication to my own growth and the meaningful work I do as a healer.

My greatest wish for you is that this book and this opportunity for healing, self-discovery, and personal growth unfolds like a masterpiece, layered with beautiful insights that awaken your soul. I wish for you incredible breakthroughs that remind you of your strength and moments so profound they make you stop and celebrate the extraordinary person you are becoming. May every step you take be filled with purpose, every discovery bring you closer to your true self, and every triumph remind you that you are worthy of all the joy, love, and success life has to offer.

Your *B.E.C.O.M.I.N.G.* starts *now.*

CHAPTER 1

The Chains that Bind

> "The first step toward freedom is learning to name the chains that have quietly shaped your life."
>
> —Monic Ayotte

Let's be real. No one sets out to live a small life.

No one dreams of waking up every day stuck in self-doubt, playing safe, or second-guessing their worth or purpose. But somehow, somewhere along the way, we get pulled under. And by the time we feel the weight, we've already convinced ourselves it's just the way life is, that change isn't possible and that we're too old to start over, too young to be taken seriously, or too broke to chase something bigger. We tell ourselves we've been in this relationship too long to walk away now or that we've invested too much in this path that we no longer want to stay on. We convince ourselves the door has closed, the window has passed, the moment is gone. But none of that is the truth. It's fear dressed up to look like reason. And it's keeping us stuck in a life that was never meant to be the final draft.

That's the power of a limiting belief.

What Is A Limiting Belief?

It is just a thought you've repeated so many times that it has stopped sounding like a story and started feeling like the truth. It starts as a thought, gets repeated as a pattern, and eventually settles in as your version of reality, the subconscious script you live by, unless you are aware of it and choose to rewrite it.

It doesn't shout. It whispers. It doesn't knock. It seeps in, quiet and familiar, until one day you find yourself living a life that doesn't feel like your own, a life shaped by fear, edited by pain, and scripted by someone else's idea of what's possible for you. These beliefs are like invisible chains, silent, sneaky, and suffocating. They show up dressed as logic, disguised as caution, and passed down like family heirlooms. "You're not ready." "You're too much." "You're not enough." And so you believe it. You shrink to fit. You trade your voice for approval and your power for belonging. You dim your light to keep others comfortable, and you bury your dreams because somewhere along the way, you were taught they were too big, too bold, too unrealistic for someone like you. I know that story, not because I read about it but because I lived it. I wore it like armor. I carried it like truth. Until one day, I realized it wasn't truth at all. It was programming. And I was allowed to rewrite it.

Let me say this again: Beliefs, empowering or limiting, aren't universal truths. They are learned. They are inherited. They are repeated. They are absolutely rewritable. They are inherited through generations, absorbed from the world around us, and installed through repetition and feeling. They are not who you are. They're just who you were taught to believe you had to be. And the moment you begin to challenge them is the moment you begin to remember your power—your power to rise, to rewrite the narrative, to reclaim the life that has always been yours, and to become who you were always meant to be.

In my own journey, limiting beliefs were like a quiet storm, wreaking havoc beneath the surface. They told me my worth was conditional, that I was only as good as what I could give to others. Somewhere along the way, I adopted the idea that my role in life was to serve, to make others happy, and to put my needs last as my truth. I became the fixer, the over-giver, the overachiever, and the ultimate people pleaser. I poured so much into everyone else that there was nothing left for myself.

At first, I couldn't see how these beliefs were quietly directing every part of my life. They were shaping my choices, feeding my fears, and defining what I thought was possible, all without me even realizing it. They were so deeply wired into my thinking, I didn't question them. I just accepted them as truth. They were like invisible rules I didn't remember agreeing to, but somehow I was living by them every single day.

But as I began to unravel the threads of my past, I realized these beliefs weren't truths at all. They were survival mechanisms, coping strategies I developed as a much younger version of myself in response to my environment.

Limiting beliefs often take root in childhood. They come from the words and actions of the people we trusted most: parents, siblings, teachers, caregivers. Maybe you had a parent who, in trying to protect you, unintentionally instilled a fear of failure. Or perhaps a teacher dismissed your potential, leaving you feeling like you'd never measure up. Worse still, maybe you grew up in an environment of chaos, where the adults around you couldn't provide the security and love you needed to feel safe. These experiences leave a mark, shaping how we see ourselves and the world.

For me, these beliefs became a survival strategy. I learned that if I was selfless enough, giving enough, and accommodating enough, I could avoid pain, discomfort and at times, I could even hold the peace, keeping the storm from breaking. I could feel a semblance of safety in a world that often felt unpredictable. But over time, those beliefs stopped serving me. They didn't protect me; they confined me. They kept me stuck in a cycle of self-sacrifice and emotional exhaustion, robbing me of the joy and fulfillment I longed for.

And that's the tricky thing about limiting beliefs; they often start as protective mechanisms. They help us cope with challenging circumstances or navigate the complexities of relationships. But as we grow up, these beliefs outlive their usefulness. They become barriers, holding us back from the freedom, success, and happiness we're capable of achieving.

The Ripple Effect of Limiting Beliefs

Limiting beliefs are like hidden currents beneath the surface of your life, subtly influencing every aspect of your reality. They ripple outwards, touching relationships, careers, health, and overall happiness. In relationships, these beliefs might convince you that you're unworthy of love or that vulnerability equals weakness. As a result, you might push people away or settle for less than you deserve, fearing rejection or pain. In the workplace, these beliefs could whisper that you're not skilled enough, stifling your ambition and causing you to shy away from opportunities for growth or advancement. This self-doubt can prevent you from taking the necessary risks to reach your professional potential, keeping you stuck in roles that don't fulfill you.

Health also feels the impact of limiting beliefs. When you believe you're not capable of change or that your efforts won't make a difference, you may neglect self-care or make choices that sabotage your well-being. This can lead to unhealthy habits that affect both your physical and mental health. Over time, these choices compound, creating a cycle that's difficult to break free from. Happiness, too, is often held hostage by these beliefs. They can cloud your perception, making it difficult to see the beauty and joy in everyday life. You might find yourself constantly striving for an unattainable ideal, never truly satisfied with what you have or who you are.

Moreover, limiting beliefs keep you stuck in a loop of fear—fear of failure, fear of judgment, or fear of the unknown. These fears become barriers that prevent you from stepping outside your comfort zone. They anchor you to a familiar but unfulfilling reality, whispering that it's safer to stay where you are. This fear can be paralyzing, causing you to miss out on experiences that could bring growth and joy. The link between limiting beliefs and mental well-being is clear. These beliefs contribute to stress, anxiety, and low self-esteem, creating a mental environment where negativity thrives. When you believe you're not good enough or that you'll never succeed, it takes a toll on your mental health. Stress levels rise, and anxiety becomes a constant companion. Low self-esteem feeds into this cycle, eroding your confidence and sense of self-worth.

The good news? These beliefs aren't permanent. They're not etched into the fabric of who you are. They're like clay, soft, malleable, and waiting to be reshaped. You have the power to change them.

The journey of transformation begins with awareness. Think of awareness as a flashlight, illuminating the dark corners of your mind where these beliefs have been hiding. With this light, you can start to examine the stories you've been telling yourself. Where did they come from? Who or what planted the seeds of these beliefs? What patterns have they created in your life?

Awareness is powerful because it leads to clarity and a profound understanding of why you think, feel, and act the way you do. When you see your beliefs for what they truly are, stories not truths, you gain the power to question them. Do they still serve you? Are they helping you become the person you want to be? If the answer is no, then it's time to rewrite them.

This process won't always feel easy or comfortable, and it's rarely a straight line. Breaking free from limiting beliefs takes courage and commitment. It takes self-compassion. And it takes a relentless willingness to face the discomfort that comes with stepping beyond what's familiar. But every brave step you take, every outdated belief you choose to question, pulls you closer to the life you were always meant to live, a life where you're no longer held hostage by fear or weighed down by self-doubt but lit up from within, grounded in purpose, and fully aligned with your truth. This isn't just healing. This is a **transformation.**

And you, my friend, are worth every second of it.

The most beautiful part of this journey is realizing you're not alone. We've all been shaped by limiting beliefs in one way or another, but we also all have the power to rise above them. You're not broken; you're human. And as a human being, you're capable of incredible growth, healing, and transformation.

So here's your invitation to begin, to shine a light on the beliefs that have been holding you back, to question their validity, and to let go of the ones that no longer serve you. This is your chance to rewrite your story, to step into the fullness of who you are, and to create a life that reflects the dreams and desires that have been stirring in your soul.

It won't happen overnight, and it won't always be easy, but I promise you this: it will be worth it. Every moment of awareness, every breakthrough, and every small victory will bring you closer to the freedom, joy, and fulfillment you were always meant to have. The chains are loosening, the walls are crumbling, and your new story is waiting to be written.

Let's get writing...

CHAPTER 2

Understanding Limiting Beliefs as a System

> "A belief is not merely an idea the mind possesses. It is an idea that possesses the mind."
>
> —Robert Oxton Bolton

Have you ever woken up with that quiet ache in your chest wondering, *"Is this really all there is?"* You go through the motions, ticking boxes, meeting expectations, but deep down something feels off, like you're living on autopilot in a life that was never fully yours. That heavy, stuck feeling? It's not laziness. It's not a lack of ambition. It's the silent grip of something deeper. It's limiting beliefs operating beneath the surface. These aren't just fleeting negative thoughts. They're subconscious patterns, deeply embedded, quietly directing your choices, shaping your identity, and reinforcing what you think is possible for your life.

They show up like invisible walls you can't see but feel constantly, walls that tell you, *"You're not smart enough," "You're not lovable,"* or *"You'll never pull that off."* And the worst part? Over time, those messages become so familiar that they start to feel like truth. Limiting beliefs act like filters, distorting your view of yourself, your worth, and your potential. You don't see the world as it is; you see it as your beliefs have taught you to see it. It becomes emotional Groundhog Day. Same fears. Same doubts. Same decisions. Different year, same cage.

But here's what most people don't realize: these beliefs are not facts. They're patterns that have been learned, absorbed, and repeated. They're part of a mental system you didn't choose, but one you have the power to change. Because if they were learned, they can be unlearned. If they were installed, they can be rewritten.

This chapter is your turning point, your invitation to begin mapping the system, recognizing the patterns, and loosening the grip of the stories that have kept you stuck. Because the life you crave, the one you've glimpsed in your quietest moments, isn't a fantasy. It's what becomes possible the moment you stop living by old beliefs and start choosing what's true.

Rooted

When working with clients, I often use the image of a tree to explain how a belief takes root and quietly begins to shape a person's entire inner world. Imagine it: the roots, the trunk, the branches, the leaves, every part connected, every part feeding the next. It all begins with a single seed. Small. Unassuming. Often unnoticed. That seed might be a careless comment, a painful experience, or a cultural message you absorbed before you were old enough to question it. But over time, that seed doesn't just sit there. It buries itself deep beneath the surface, anchoring into your subconscious and growing quietly, relentlessly.

The roots of that belief form beneath your awareness, the early memories, interactions, and impressions that gave it life. Maybe it began the day a teacher overlooked your potential. Or the moment a parent, without meaning to, made their love feel conditional. Those moments don't just pass through you, they stay. They dig in. And those roots spread, becoming the foundation of what starts to feel like truth.

Then comes the trunk, the solid, central narrative you eventually accept as fact. It might sound like *"I'm not good enough," "I don't belong,"* or *"I'll never be truly loved."* This trunk becomes sturdy, inflexible. A fixed belief that holds up everything else. You stop seeing it as a possibility… and start living as if it's a certainty.

From there, branches begin to grow. These are the stories you tell yourself to support the belief, the evidence you gather to keep it alive. If the trunk says *"I'm not good enough,"* a branch might whisper, *"That failed project proves it."* Another might say, *"No one ever really sees me."* These stories become the lens through which you view your world, each one looping back to the same unexamined core.

And then there's the leaves, the thoughts, emotions, and behaviors that stem from it all. The leaves are what the world sees, but they're only the surface. That belief of *"I'm not lovable"* might show up as anxiety in relationships, self-sabotage, or an instinct to push people away before they get too close. Sadness, withdrawal, overachievement, perfectionism… these are the outward expressions of a system rooted in fear and shaped by the past.

This metaphor helps us see what most people miss: a belief isn't just a thought, it's a living system. A structure. A pattern. Each part—root, trunk, branch, and leaf—interconnected and reinforcing the others. That's why change takes more than just positive thinking. You have to explore the whole system. You begin by noticing the leaves and branches: *What am I feeling? What am I doing? What stories am I telling myself?* Then you trace those stories back to the trunk: *What belief is holding all of this together?* And finally, you dig deep, down to the roots: *Where did this even begin? Is it true? Do I still want to carry it?*

Because once you see the whole tree for what it is, you realize something powerful: **What was planted can be uprooted. What was learned can be unlearned. And what was shaping you… can be rewritten.**

True transformation begins when you have the courage to reach beneath the surface and start pulling the belief out by its roots. Because when the roots go, everything else begins to fall away. The trunk loses its strength. The branches crack. The leaves, those patterns, reactions, and behaviors you've carried for years, begin to wither and drop.

And in that sacred space where the old system once stood, something beautiful happens: you get to plant something new—a new seed, one rooted not in fear or lack but in self-worth, in possibility, in the truth of who you're becoming. And just like before, it starts small. But this time, it grows with intention. With love. With power. As you nurture it, the roots take hold, not to keep you stuck but to ground you in your truth. The trunk grows strong with resilience. The branches stretch toward your potential. The leaves bloom with actions, thoughts, and emotions that actually serve you.

The tree becomes a symbol of your inner world, alive, evolving, and fully yours.

And that's the beautiful thing about beliefs. They're not set in stone. They're not your destiny. They're living systems, which means they can be pruned, reshaped, uprooted, and completely rebuilt. And when you begin to understand your beliefs this way—one root, one branch, one leaf at a time—you reclaim your power to choose, to grow on purpose, and to become who you were always meant to be.

And as your new tree rises, taller, stronger, aligned with your truth, you'll look back and realize: this was never about the old story. It was always about planting something better.

Core Beliefs vs. Seed Beliefs

To truly transform your mindset, you have to understand the architecture of your beliefs, the system behind the thoughts that hold you back. One of the most powerful ways to explore this is through the metaphor of a tree because every belief system, just like every tree, starts with a seed.

Picture it: a small, quiet seed, barely noticeable. It was planted by an experience, a comment, or a moment you didn't even realize left a mark. That seed takes hold and sends down roots. Deep ones. Those roots form beneath the surface, anchoring into your subconscious where they quietly shape how you think and feel. From the roots grows a trunk, strong, central, and foundational. It becomes the core belief, the main storyline you begin to live by. From there, branches stretch out in every direction. These are the stories and assumptions that support the core belief. And finally, the leaves appear: your day-to-day thoughts, emotions, and behaviors. What people *see* is just the surface. What's underneath? That's where the real work begins.

This belief tree gives you a powerful framework. Because if you want to change the fruit, you have to dig up the root. Let's break this down even further:

Core Beliefs—The Trunk and Branches of Your Mindset

Core beliefs are the solid trunk of your internal world, the central narratives you've come to believe about yourself, others, and life. They feel absolute. They shape how you interpret your experiences, how you show up in relationships, how you handle failure, and what you believe you deserve.

Core beliefs are:

- **Broad and sweeping.** They sound like unshakable truths:
  "I'm not good enough."
  "The world is against me."
  "People can't be trusted."
- **Persistent.** They stick around for years, reinforced over and over until they become second nature.
- **Life-shaping.** They influence your confidence, your decisions, your relationships, your limits, and what you allow yourself to hope for.

Some common core beliefs might be:

- *I'm unworthy of love or success.*
- *I'll never be good enough.*
- *I'm too old to change now.*

These beliefs are the "truths" you've accepted without realizing they were ever optional. But they are. You weren't born with them. They grew from somewhere, and that somewhere is what we call **the seed.**

Seed Beliefs—The Roots Beneath the Surface

Every core belief begins with a seed: a moment, a message, a memory. Often, this happens in childhood, when our minds are wide open and eager to make sense of the world. These seed beliefs form when something painful, confusing, or repetitive happens, and we assign it meaning.

Seed beliefs are:

- **Specific in origin.** They come from real moments:
  A teacher telling you, *"You're just not cut out for this."* A parent withholding affection unless you performed or behaved a certain way. A painful rejection that whispered, *"You don't belong."*
- **Emotionally charged.** They carry weight because they were tied to a deep emotional wound or unmet need.
- **The blueprint for bigger beliefs.** One seed can grow into a whole forest of limiting narratives if left unchecked.

Examples of seed beliefs might include:

- Failing once and deciding, *"I'm not smart."*
- Being left out and internalizing, *"I'm not wanted."*
- Constantly being criticized and concluding, *"I'm a failure."*

These seeds burrow deep. They become the roots, feeding the core beliefs and quietly dictating your self-image, your relationships, your choices, and your dreams.

How Core and Seed Beliefs Work Together

You can't heal the tree by trimming the leaves. You have to go deeper.

If you only focus on the symptoms, the leaves and branches, you'll never uproot what's truly holding you back. That's why transformation requires us to trace the core belief back to the seed. You dig. You investigate. You ask, *Where did this belief begin? Who told me this? Is it even true?*

Let's say your core belief is *"I'm not worthy of love."* When you trace it back, you realize the seed was planted in childhood, when a parent withheld affection unless you were perfect, quiet, or helpful.

Or maybe your core belief is *"I'm not capable of success."* And the seed? A moment when someone you trusted said, *"Don't aim too high. You'll just be disappointed."*

Once you identify the seed, you take away the root system that's been feeding the lie. And in its place? You plant something new—a belief that reflects who you are now not who you were then, a belief that's rooted in self-worth, possibility, and truth.

Why This Matters

Understanding the difference between core beliefs and seed beliefs isn't just a helpful insight, it's the gateway to lasting, soul-deep transformation. This isn't about theory. It's about freedom. Because here's the truth: if you don't know where your limiting beliefs come from, you'll spend your life trimming branches while the roots keep growing back stronger. You'll keep repeating the same patterns, making the same choices, feeling the same stuckness, and wondering why nothing ever truly changes.

Core beliefs are the invisible rules you've been living by, the unspoken "truths" that have shaped your identity. But they aren't facts. They're habits of thought, inherited and reinforced over time. And seed beliefs? They're where it all begins. Those early, often painful moments where something was said, withheld, or misunderstood, planting the seeds of self-doubt, fear, and unworthiness. And unless we go back and challenge them, those seeds grow, shaping how we see ourselves, how we love (or don't love), and how we live.

And here's what I know for sure: **we live our lives according to what we believe.** I've seen it in my clients, and I've lived it in my own story. These beliefs become the lens through which we view the world and ourselves, and that lens influences *everything.*

When you uncover these beliefs, when you name them, trace them, and question them, you begin to reclaim your power. Imagine your limiting beliefs as a tree that's been dominating your inner landscape for years, its roots tangled deep in your subconscious, its branches casting shadows over everything you want. By going to the source, not just chopping at symptoms but pulling the whole belief system out by the roots, you create space. Space to breathe. Space to dream. Space to grow something new.

Because your beliefs shape everything. They're the filter through which you see the world. If you believe *"I'm not good enough,"* you'll unconsciously build a life that matches that belief. You'll play small. You'll second-guess yourself. You'll tolerate less than you deserve. But when you challenge that belief, when you find its root and realize it was never your truth, that it was just a story, you unlock the door to profound, liberating change.

Think about it: every decision you make, every risk you take (or don't), every relationship you hold onto or walk away from, it all flows through your belief system. And if that system is limited, so is your life. But when your beliefs become empowering, everything shifts. Your mindset becomes a launchpad, not a cage. You stop surviving. You start rising. You ***become*** who you were always meant to be.

This work matters because *you* matter. Your potential has always been there. It's just been hidden beneath the weight of old beliefs that never belonged to you in the first place. And when you finally decide to do the work, when you choose to face the roots instead of just managing the symptoms, you give yourself something priceless: permission—permission to change, permission to let go, permission to become.

Yes, this process takes courage. Yes, it demands honesty, vulnerability, and persistence. But the reward? It's everything. It's a life where you're no longer defined by who you've been, but inspired by who you're becoming. It's a life where your beliefs don't hold you back, they lift you higher.

So the question isn't whether you're capable of transformation. The question is, *Are you ready to uproot the old and plant something new?*

Get your shovel. Let's get digging… Next chapter!

CHAPTER 3

Neural Makeover

The Brain Science Behind Breaking Free From Limiting Beliefs

> "Neurons that fire together wire together."
>
> —Donald Hebb,
> Canadian neuropsychologist
> and pioneer of neuroplasticity

Understanding the science behind limiting beliefs opens up a whole new world of insight, so let's have a peek behind the curtain!

Beliefs don't just exist in your mind. They are physically embedded in your brain's structure. And this isn't just metaphorical. When we form beliefs, our brains actually create new neural pathways to support those thoughts. Think of these pathways like highways in your brain, and each time you think a thought or reinforce a belief, you're adding more lanes to the highway, making the path faster and more automatic. This is where neuroscience really gets fascinating. According to Dr.

Joe Dispenza, "The brain is a record of the past." Every thought, every experience, and every belief you've ever had is etched into your neural networks. Your brain's job is to create a record of all those experiences, and the more frequently you think a particular thought, the more it strengthens that neural network. This becomes the "default setting" of your brain. The more you tell yourself "I'm not good enough," for example, the more your brain solidifies that belief into a fast lane of neural connections, making it feel like an undeniable truth.

Here's where it gets even more interesting. Neuroscientists call this process neuroplasticity, which is the brain's ability to reorganize itself by forming new neural connections. This is exciting because it means that your brain isn't stuck. It's not a fixed, rigid structure—far from it. In fact, as Dr. Dispenza explains, "The brain is capable of changing and rewiring itself as a result of our thinking." In simple terms: You can teach your brain new tricks. Let's use a quick analogy to help visualize this. Imagine you've been walking down the same dirt path in the woods for years. The more you walk that path, the more it becomes a well-trodden trail. Eventually, the ground gets worn down, and the path becomes deeply ingrained in the landscape. But, if you decide one day to walk a different path, you might feel awkward at first because it's not as familiar, it's overgrown, and it's a little uncomfortable. But with repeated effort, that new path starts to form, and the old, familiar trail begins to fade. You can think of limiting beliefs as the well-worn trail and empowering beliefs as the new path. Every time you challenge your old beliefs and take a step forward in a new direction, you're creating new neural pathways in your brain.

This is neurogenesis in action. It's your brain's ability to create new neurons, or brain cells, based on your experiences. As you begin to think and act in ways that challenge your old limiting beliefs, you're actually creating new neural cells that support these new ways of thinking. This process is the key to rewiring your brain and creating a new reality. It's like turning the page of an old book and writing a new chapter.

But here's the catch: this brain rewiring doesn't happen automatically. It requires focused attention and effort. Dr. Dispenza emphasizes the importance of mindful repetition in this process. "To change your life, you have to change your energy–to change your energy, you have to change your state of being," he claims. In other words, just thinking about a new belief isn't enough. You have to fully embody it. That means living and acting as if that new belief is already true. The more you focus on this new belief, the more you engage with it emotionally and physically, the faster your brain will rewire itself to support that belief.

And let's not forget about quantum physics (yes, we're going there!). Dr. Dispenza draws a connection between quantum physics and brain rewiring. He suggests that when you change your thoughts, you're essentially shifting your energy frequency, which in turn shifts your reality. Your brain operates on an electromagnetic frequency, and when you introduce new thoughts and beliefs, you're altering the way your brain emits energy. This new energy, in turn, influences the way you interact with the world around you. So when you consistently replace limiting beliefs with empowering ones, you not only change your brain but also change your relationship with the world. Here's the bottom line: you are not stuck in your old beliefs. The science is clear. Your brain is capable of incredible transformation. You can rewire your brain, shift your energy, and create new neural pathways that support empowering beliefs. And the more you practice this, the more natural it becomes, just like walking down a new, well-established path in the woods.

So the next time you catch yourself thinking, "I'm not good enough" or "I'll never make it," remember that belief is just a well-worn path in your brain. You have the power to create a new one; it's just a matter of putting in the effort, challenging your old beliefs, and consistently reinforcing the new ones. As Dr. Dispenza so powerfully says, "The only way to create a new reality is to change the thoughts and emotions that create that reality."

And here's the best part: I've got just the thing to help you make it happen! The B.E.C.O.M.I.N.G. Formula! It is your personalized blueprint for rewiring your brain, embracing your full potential, and unlocking a life full of possibility. It's not a one-size-fits-all solution but a powerful, step-by-step process designed to help you break free from those limiting beliefs and guide you toward the life you're truly meant to live. Think of it as your mental-makeover toolkit, ready to equip you with everything you need to shift your mindset and start creating the life you deserve.

Before we jump into the formula, let's take a moment to explore a bit more of the science behind it all. Trust me, it'll be worth it!

Why Your Mind Believes What It Believes

Your Brain's Personal Bouncer: Meet the RAS

Here's where things get wild, in a good way. Deep in your brainstem is a small but mighty system called the **Reticular Activating System**, or **RAS** for short. Sounds fancy, right? Think of it as your brain's personal bouncer. It decides what information gets through to your conscious mind and what gets politely shown the door.

The RAS is constantly scanning your environment, sorting through a flood of data, and choosing what to highlight based on what it *thinks* is important. And what does it use to make those decisions? You guessed it! Your beliefs.

If you've been carrying around the belief of *"I'm not good enough,"* your RAS will get right to work filtering the world through that lens. It'll highlight every awkward silence in a conversation, the typo in your email, or the time someone forgot your name and say, *"See? Told you so."* It confirms what you believe, **not what's true**.

But here's the powerful twist: when you begin shifting your beliefs, even just slightly, your RAS changes its filter. Say you start leaning into *"I am worthy and capable,"* your RAS gets the memo. It starts flagging the compliment your coworker gave you, the task you nailed, or the smile from a stranger as evidence of this new belief. It's like your brain says, *"Ah, this is what we're focusing on now. Got it."*

This is why **reprogramming your beliefs** (like with the B.E.C.O.M.I.N.G. Formula) is so powerful. When you change what your brain tags as important, you literally begin to see a different world.

The takeaway? Your RAS is always working for you, but it can only serve the beliefs you feed it. So if you don't like what your brain's been showing you, it's time to give your bouncer a new guest list.

How Beliefs Are Maintained: RAS and Confirmation Bias

Now that you understand the role of the Reticular Activating System (RAS), let's explore another key player in how your beliefs are formed and reinforced: **confirmation bias**. Together, these two mental processes shape how you see yourself and the world, often without you even realizing it.

Both RAS and confirmation bias are constantly working in the background, helping your brain decide what to notice and how to interpret it. And while that might sound helpful, the problem is this: they don't care whether a belief is true or empowering. They just care that it's familiar.

The Reticular Activating System (RAS)

As you now know, the RAS is a bundle of nerves in your brainstem that acts like a filter, deciding which pieces of information are important enough to grab your attention. It's always scanning your environment for what aligns with your beliefs and what you tend to focus on most.

For example, if you believe *"my body is too fat"* or *"my body is too skinny,"* your RAS will start pointing out things that seem to confirm that belief, a passing glance you interpret as judgment, a fitness post on social media that triggers comparison, or a moment of self-consciousness in the mirror. Meanwhile, the compliments you receive, the moments you feel strong, or the progress you've made might get completely overlooked. Your brain isn't trying to hurt you, it just thinks it's helping by spotlighting what you've been focused on the most.

The more attention a belief gets, the stronger and more automatic this filter becomes.

Confirmation Bias

While your RAS decides what gets your attention, confirmation bias is how your mind makes sense of what you notice. It's the mental shortcut that makes you pay more attention to things that support what you already believe and ignore or dismiss anything that doesn't.

So if you believe *"my body is too fat,"* confirmation bias will zoom in on the way your jeans fit on a bloated day or a photo you didn't like of yourself. It'll have you replay that one comment someone made five years ago. And it will downplay or completely forget the moments you felt confident, the genuine compliments from others, or the way your body shows up for you every single day.

How They Work Together

Here's where it gets tricky: your RAS brings in the information, and confirmation bias gives it meaning, all in a way that backs up your belief. Over time, this creates a powerful loop that keeps that belief alive, even when it's untrue or harmful. If the belief is disempowering, the cycle can keep you stuck. But the good news? Once you understand the loop, you can interrupt it. You can start telling your brain what to look for. You can choose beliefs that empower you, and your brain will eventually start noticing the proof.

But here's the incredible opportunity: now that you understand how this system works, you can begin to change it, intentionally and powerfully. By choosing new, empowering beliefs and reinforcing them through your thoughts, actions, and emotions, you can retrain your brain's filters to seek out truth, strength, and possibility. Instead of replaying the old narratives that kept you stuck, you begin to shift your entire internal landscape toward what you actually want to create.

This is where true transformation begins. You are not a prisoner of your past programming. With awareness as your guide, you have the power to rewrite the story. You can reshape the lens through which you see yourself and open the door to a future that finally feels like yours.

And this is exactly where the B.E.C.O.M.I.N.G. Formula comes in. It's not just a framework, it's a blueprint for mental and emotional rewiring. It's a step-by-step, science-based, soul-aligned system designed to help you identify the beliefs that have been holding you back and replace them with the ones that push you forward. If you're ready to stop surviving and start thriving, the B.E.C.O.M.I.N.G. Formula is your invitation. This is the path.

But first… a little more science. Because the more you understand the functioning behind it all, the more power you have to transform your life from the inside out. Keep reading. What comes next isn't just science, it's a revelation that could completely change the way you relate to your brilliant, beautiful brain.

The Silent Architect: How Your Subconscious Shapes Your Story

Let's talk about how your subconscious mind plays into all of this because understanding this part of your brain is like finding the hidden blueprint to why you think, feel, and behave the way you do.

The subconscious mind is a master archivist. It stores every experience, every emotion, and every belief you've ever picked up (especially from childhood), cataloging them and using them as reference points for how to keep you safe. And safety is the key word here. Your subconscious mind has one primary job: to move you away from pain and toward pleasure. But, and this is important, it doesn't distinguish between what is healthy and what is harmful, between what empowers you and what keeps you small. It only cares about what feels familiar and safe.

As a child, you developed subconscious strategies for coping with fear, pain, shame, or rejection. Maybe you learned to hide your emotions, people-please, withdraw, overachieve, or seek control, anything that offered a sense of relief or protection. These coping mechanisms, though often maladaptive in adulthood, were simply your subconscious doing its job: keeping you out of perceived danger and discomfort.

In my own journey, this understanding was a game-changer. For decades, I struggled with eating disorders and body dysmorphia. On the outside, it may have looked like control or discipline, but underneath, it was my subconscious trying to shield me from deeper emotional pain. It was trying to protect me from feelings of inadequacy, rejection, and fear by offering me a sense of control, no matter how destructive that control was.

When I began to uncover these subconscious patterns, everything shifted. I realized I wasn't broken; I was programmed. My brain had simply learned ways to survive that no longer served me. That realization didn't just lead to healing, it lit a fire in me. I became fascinated with the subconscious mind, which led me to pursue hypnosis. Why? Because hypnosis speaks the language of the subconscious. It bypasses the critical mind and allows us to rewire those old, outdated beliefs at their root.

So when you start to understand how your subconscious has been working to protect you, you gain something priceless: compassion for yourself. You see the choices you made not as flaws but as strategies. And most importantly, you realize that those strategies can be changed. You are not stuck. You are not broken. You are ready to rewire.

And the formula is not just a process, it's a powerful framework for transforming the patterns that have held you back. It helps you retrain your brain, reprogram your subconscious, and replace survival strategies with ones that actually support your growth, your joy, and your worth.

This isn't about becoming someone new. It's about becoming who you were always meant to be, before the world told you otherwise.

Self-Sabotage: When Safety Disguises Itself as Struggle

So let's bring it all together.

At this point, you've seen how your beliefs aren't just fleeting thoughts, they're deeply wired into your brain. You've explored how the Reticular Activating System and confirmation bias filter your reality based on those beliefs. You've peeked beneath the surface and glimpsed the subconscious mind, the silent driver that's been steering your life not based on what's true or empowering but based on what once felt *safe.* And this... this is where self-sabotage sneaks in wearing the mask of protection.

Let's say you've carried a subconscious belief since childhood that you're not worthy of love unless you *earn* it by being perfect, selfless, or endlessly accommodating. Maybe you watched your parents model dysfunction, or maybe love was conditional, tied to performance or obedience. So your subconscious, doing what it's wired to do, avoid pain and move toward safety, tucks that belief away and builds behaviors around it. It doesn't ask if it's healthy. It only asks, *Will this keep us safe? Will this keep us loved?*

Now fast forward to your adult relationships. You find yourself in the same painful dynamic again and again: overgiving, losing your voice, staying too long in toxic partnerships, or sabotaging the healthy ones that feel unfamiliar. Not because you're broken. Not because you want chaos. But because, to your subconscious, that chaos is *predictable.* Conditional love is *familiar.* That old pain is the devil you know, and the unknown feels riskier than the suffering you've normalized.

This is self-sabotage in action. Not a character flaw. Not a lack of willpower. It's simply your subconscious trying to protect you with outdated programming. It's reenacting the past because, somewhere deep inside, it equates *safety* with the known, even when the known hurts.

But now… you know better. You see it.

This is the moment you take your power back. Because once you name it, you can reframe it. You can teach your brain and your subconscious a new definition of safety, one rooted in worthiness, joy, peace, and healthy connection. You can rewire your mind, rewrite your beliefs, and redefine what love and success look like for you.

Step by step, belief by belief, we're going to gently pull up the roots, clear the path, and plant something new, something aligned with your truth, not your trauma. So, are you ready?

Now that we've explored how your subconscious mind, belief systems, and brain wiring have been quietly scripting your life behind the scenes, it's time to turn our focus to the next part of the journey.

This next chapter is about looking back, not to relive the past but to understand how it's been shaping your present and quietly influencing your future. Because the truth is your past isn't just behind you… it's within you in the beliefs you've inherited, the stories you've carried, and the patterns you've repeated without even realizing it.

But don't be afraid. This isn't about blame, shame, or picking at old scars. It's about awareness, compassion, and growth. This is your opportunity to see yourself clearly, not critically, and to understand the "why" behind the patterns, so you can finally choose differently and step into the life you truly desire.

This is the part of the framework where healing deepens, awareness sharpens, and your sense of becoming expands. Get ready to uncover the hidden threads that connect your past to your present and to finally decide how the next chapter of your becoming will unfold.

Let's go!

CHAPTER 4

The Blueprint Beneath

How Beliefs Are Born

"Your past may explain you, but it doesn't define you."

— Dr. Thema Bryant

I know you're eager to dive in, to start shifting, changing, and becoming, and that excitement is the spark we need. But before we build something extraordinary, we need to lay a solid foundation. To truly break free, we must first understand the whys and hows, the roots of limiting beliefs, the brain's brilliant but protective wiring, and the subconscious patterns that have kept you stuck. When you understand how your mind works, you gain the power to change it. This chapter is where we layer on the understanding because knowledge isn't just power, it's liberation.

The Blueprint

Every story has a beginning. Yours started long before you had words to tell it, etched not in ink, but in emotion. Long before you could speak your truth, the world was already whispering its version of who you should be. Those early whispers became blueprints.

The architecture of your beliefs didn't begin with conscious thought. It began with how you felt, what you sensed, and how the world responded to your existence. Your caregivers, your culture, your environment—all of them left impressions, not in your intellect but in your nervous system. And because the part of your brain responsible for logic, emotional regulation, and critical thinking wasn't fully developed yet, those impressions went in unfiltered.

This is the **inductive stage of learning**, where as children, we aren't reasoning yet, we are absorbing. We aren't questioning, we are internalizing. We don't think, *"Is this true?"* We think, *"This must be who I am."*

A child doesn't understand that a stressed-out parent is struggling with their own inner demons. A child sees a withdrawn face or a harsh tone and thinks, *"What did I do wrong?"* They make it about themselves, not because they're self-centered but because their brain is designed that way.

Dr. Gabor Maté puts it perfectly:

> **"Children are the ultimate narcissists, not in the negative sense of the word but in the sense that their world revolves around them. They believe they are the cause of everything that happens to them, both good and bad."**

And that belief, if left unchallenged, becomes the seedbed of limiting beliefs.

The Stories We Inherit Without Consent

Imagine a child whose every mistake is met with criticism. Over time, they don't hear feedback, they hear failure. The message becomes, *"I can't do anything right."* That belief doesn't fade with age. It matures with them, woven into their identity like background noise they stop noticing but always hear.

Or the child whose problems are solved by an anxious caregiver before they can even try to come up with a solution to their discomfort. They grow up thinking, "*The world is dangerous. I'm not capable.*" Not because anyone said those words but because they were modeled, reinforced, felt.

And then there are the homes marked by addiction, volatility, and abuse, where love is inconsistent and fear is constant. These children become emotional detectives, reading tone, scanning faces, and sensing energy shifts. Their nervous system becomes their guide, not curiosity, not joy. And they learn, quietly and deeply: "*My feelings aren't safe. My needs are too much. I am too much.*"

These aren't just memories, they're programs. Installations. They're early survival adaptations that helped them cope then, but keep them trapped now. Let me show you what I mean.

When Childhood Pain Grows Up

A child grows up in a home marked by emotional abuse, perhaps with a parent who explodes unpredictably, belittles them, or uses love as a weapon. That child learns, very quickly, how to read the room. They become hypervigilant. They study facial expressions, tones, and footsteps. They walk on eggshells, adjusting their behavior constantly in an attempt to avoid the next outburst. And because their brain is still in survival mode, still egocentric, they don't think, "*My parent is wounded.*" They think, "*This is happening because of me.*"

Fast forward 20, 30, even 40 years, and that same child is now an adult. They may be wildly successful or constantly struggling. They may be a high achiever or paralyzed by self-doubt. But underneath the surface, that same survival programming is still running the show. They may:

- **Over-apologize** in relationships, even when they've done nothing wrong.
- **Avoid confrontation** at all costs, believing conflict means danger.
- **Sabotage healthy connections** because love doesn't feel safe, it feels suspicious.
- **Struggle with boundaries**, believing saying no will make them unlovable or provoke punishment.
- **Overachieve** to prove their worth or underperform because they've internalized they're not good enough.

I've seen these patterns again and again. I've had clients coming in with shame, burnout, anxiety, addiction, or perfectionism, not realizing that beneath it all is a scared inner child still trying to avoid being hurt.

And this doesn't just show up in trauma survivors. It appears in high-functioning professionals, exhausted caregivers, burned-out parents, and brilliant creatives who keep holding themselves back. Because when you believe, on a subconscious level, that you're not worthy, that your needs are too much, or that love must be earned through self-sacrifice, you will shape your entire life around those beliefs.

Patterns, Not Flaws

This is not about shame or blame. This is about **understanding**.

You are not broken. You are patterned. And patterns can be rewritten.

When you understand that your beliefs were formed in an environment where your brain was trying to protect you, it changes the game. What once felt like character flaws or failures begin to reveal themselves as survival strategies—smart, creative, deeply human responses to a world that didn't always feel safe.

The belief that you have to earn love? A response to conditional affection. The belief that your voice doesn't matter? A reaction to being ignored or dismissed. The belief that chaos is normal? A mirror of your earliest environment. But you're not there anymore. And you don't have to live like you are.

The Cultural Web

It's not just our families who shape us, it's also the society we're steeped in. Culture, media, religion, education… all send powerful messages about what it means to be enough.

You don't have to experience trauma to develop limiting beliefs. All you have to do is grow up in a world that constantly tells you to be different. Shrink here. Perform there. Be quiet. Lose weight. Be productive. Don't cry. Don't fail.

These messages aren't neutral. They're insidious. They sneak into our subconscious through repetition and reward. And suddenly, we're carrying beliefs we never agreed to, living lives that don't reflect who we are but who we were told to be.

And when those messages clash with your soul's truth, you feel it. That restlessness? That burnout? That deep, aching sense that you were made for something more? That's your truth rising up through the noise, trying to get your attention.

The Math Seed

As a child, I wore overachievement like armor. I chased perfection with relentless energy, craving the kind of validation that made me feel like I mattered. My self-worth clung to praise, gold stars, and glowing report cards. And being the "good girl" became the currency of my enoughness. As long as I excelled academically, I felt seen. I felt worthy. I felt safe.

But then came middle school, and everything began to unravel. Puberty ushered in a tidal wave of insecurity I wasn't ready for. My body changed, and with it, the way I saw myself changed. Every glance in the mirror deepened a discomfort I couldn't name but always felt. The teasing started early: comments about my weight that seemed casual to others but hit me like a wrecking ball. Each one planted seeds of shame, which quickly grew into the belief that my worth was tied to how I looked. And in a world where beauty standards were cruel and narrow, I never measured up.

By the time I hit middle school, I was already convinced something was wrong with me. So I did what I had always done, I doubled down. If I couldn't be beautiful, maybe I could be brilliant. Maybe if I just worked harder, performed better, achieved more, I could outrun the shame.

But then came science class. For the first time, my efforts didn't yield results. I struggled to understand the material, and instead of support, I got dismissal. My teacher didn't offer encouragement; he offered conclusions. "Science just isn't your thing," he said. "It's normal for girls to struggle." He even told my parents I wasn't putting in enough effort, reinforcing the idea that my failure wasn't about circumstance; it was about me. I didn't have the tools back then to question his bias. I didn't see that he was projecting his own limitations onto me. I just internalized it, like I always had. "*You're not good at science. You're not good enough.*"

The following year, I had a teacher who wasn't just unsupportive, he was someone whose true nature I'd only come to understand much later: he was a predator. As fate would have it, he taught both math and gym, two areas where I struggled to feel confident since the seed of inadequacy had firmly rooted. At 13 years old, I couldn't fully comprehend his inappropriate and neglectful behavior toward students, especially those who didn't fit into his narrow mold of "worthy."

I was mediocre in gym class at best and struggling in math, falling far short of what would earn his approval. I certainly wasn't one of the pretty or popular girls who seemed to gain his attention effortlessly. To him, I wasn't a star athlete or an academic prodigy. I was just another student in need of help, a burden requiring more than he cared to give.

When years later details of his predatory behavior were made public, my reaction shocked even myself. Instead of feeling anger or disgust, my first thought was a crushing wave of shame. I wasn't even worthy of his attention. I was not even enough to be noticed by someone like *him.*

Ponder that one for a moment, if you will! That's how deeply my limiting beliefs had warped my sense of self.

By high school, the narrative was fully cemented. In grade ten, a math teacher delivered what felt like the final blow. He told me if I never took another class with him again, he would give me a passing grade. The words were sharp, and the message was clear: "*You're too much. You ask too many questions. You're not worth the effort.*" That experience didn't just kill my confidence, it buried it. And it left behind a story I would carry for years: "*You're a burden. You're incapable. Don't even bother.*"

By the time I reached university, I didn't just believe I was bad at math, I believed I was hopeless. I failed and retook multiple methodology courses, each one reinforcing the narrative I had absorbed as truth.

And I know, on the surface, this might sound like just another academic struggle. To some, fearing math may even seem trivial or exaggerated. But let me tell you, it wasn't. The emotional pain I carried from believing I was a failure in this area ran deep. This wasn't just about numbers or formulas. This was about self-worth. About capability. About my right to belong in spaces I once thought were off limits to girls like me. The shame was so strong, the fear so consuming, it nearly derailed my academic goals not once but over and over as a teenager, as a student, and even as a teacher. The emotional stress it caused was real. It affected my confidence, my choices, my health, and my belief in what was possible for me.

Until life handed me a turning point.

It came years later in grad school: a graduate-level methodology course, staring back at me from the syllabus like a ghost I hadn't yet exorcised. I froze. Panic overtook me. And just like that, I was thirteen again, awkward, invisible, and drowning in shame. My first assignment? A disaster. I failed spectacularly. And for a brief moment I thought, "*See? They were right all along.*"

But something had changed. *I* had changed.

By then, I had done the work. I had unpacked my story, sat with the discomfort, and met the frightened child inside me with compassion and truth. I had learned how to separate fact from programming. I had realized that *this belief wasn't mine to carry.* It had been handed to me, shaped by other people's wounds and biases. But I didn't have to keep living by it.

So I didn't. I made a different choice. I asked for help. I used every resource I could find. I leaned into the discomfort and kept showing up, not to prove anything to anyone else but to finally prove to *myself* that I was never the problem. Every day, I reminded myself with a mantra that became my lifeline:

> **"Sister, you've got this. You always get it done, you're just that person that gets shit done."**
>
> **–Monic Ayotte**

And I believed it. I didn't just pass the course, I crushed it with a grade of 85%. But you know what? The grade wasn't the win. The true victory was reclaiming my narrative. I didn't just rewrite the story, I burned the old one and started fresh, pen in hand, voice intact. Here's what I want you to know:

- Your limiting beliefs are not facts.
- Your past does not get to decide your future.
- And the stories you've been handed?
  You don't have to keep them.

And every time you choose to rise, to question, to rewrite, you give others permission to do the same. That is the real ripple effect of healing. That is how we change the world, not by being perfect but by becoming free.

The Shift

Healing doesn't mean erasing your past. It means decoding it. It's about looking at your story with compassion and context, not shame or blame. It's standing in front of the mirror and whispering, "Oh... that's why." Because it wasn't just your thoughts that were shaped in childhood, your nervous system was shaped, too. Long before you had words to describe what was happening around you, your body was already keeping score. If your early environment felt chaotic, critical, emotionally distant, or unpredictable, your nervous system adapted, and it did so brilliantly. It learned to scan the room before you even walked in. It learned that shrinking made you less of a target. It learned that saying "yes" was safer than saying "no" and that staying quiet might keep the peace. It learned to shut down emotionally when feelings became too overwhelming to carry.

These weren't dysfunctional responses. They were survival strategies.

Hypervigilance? That was your body saying, "Stay alert. Something could go wrong at any moment." Emotional numbing? "Better not feel this. It's too much." People pleasing? "Maybe if I take care of everyone else I'll be safe or even loved."

These aren't flaws in your character. And for a time, they worked. But the nervous system doesn't automatically update when life moves on. Unless we intentionally rewire it, the body continues to react to today with the fears of yesterday. It's like your mind is trying to move forward, but your body is still stuck in the old story, waiting for the next blow.

That's why healing isn't just about changing your thoughts. It's about showing your body, gently and consistently, that it's finally safe—safe to rest, safe to feel, safe to stop bracing for impact, safe to belong, and safe to take up space. That kind of healing? That's the kind that changes everything. Because in those moments, when your nervous system no longer believes it has to fight, flee, or freeze, you reclaim something that was taken from you a long time ago: choice.

You get to pause. You get to question. You get to ask "*Does this belief still serve me? Who gave it to me? Do I still want to carry it forward?*"

That's where your power begins to return. And that's where your real story begins.

Your Becoming Begins Here

The fact that you're reading this, showing up for this work, means something is shifting already. You are becoming the person your younger self needed. You are choosing awareness over autopilot. You are unlearning what no longer serves and reclaiming what was always yours: your worth, your power, your truth.

This is not about perfection. It's about liberation. It's not about blaming the past. It's about transforming it. It's not about becoming someone new. It's about remembering who you've always been.

You are not the stories that hurt you.
You are not the beliefs that limit you.
You are not the survival strategies that once kept you safe.

You are more.

Now that you understand the blueprint, it's time to reclaim the pen. The next chapter is yours to write, with truth, with courage, and with the unshakable belief that you are no longer defined by your past but empowered by your **becoming**.

CHAPTER 5

The Body Remembers

How Your Nervous System Protects and Limits You

> "Your nervous system isn't broken. It's brilliant.
> It adapted to keep you safe even when 'safe'
> meant staying small."
>
> —Monic Ayotte

Before we dive into the B.E.C.O.M.I.N.G. Formula, the transformational path to breaking free from limiting beliefs and stepping into your truest, most powerful self, there's one more truth you need to hear, one that ties everything together:

Transformation isn't just a mindset shift. It's a *nervous system* shift. So what exactly do we mean when we say "nervous system"?

Your nervous system is the part of your body responsible for processing everything you experience. It's your body's communication highway, sending signals between your brain, your spinal cord, and every other part of your body. It controls how you respond to the world around you, your reactions, your heart rate, your breathing, your stress levels, and your sense of safety. It's always working, even when you're unaware of it, scanning your environment and interpreting whether you're safe or under threat.

There are two main branches of your nervous system: the **sympathetic**, which activates your fight, flight, freeze, or **fawn responses**, and the **parasympathetic**, which helps you rest, digest, and feel grounded and safe.

Most of us are familiar with fight, flight, or freeze, but **fawn** is the quieter survival strategy. It often develops in environments where staying safe means staying agreeable. It's the reflex to please, appease, or accommodate, smoothing things over, avoiding conflict, and putting others' needs ahead of your own. It's how your nervous system learned to protect you by staying invisible, likable, or easy to love.

None of these responses are wrong. They're not signs of weakness. They're signs of a nervous system doing its job: keeping you alive. But when you've lived through chronic stress, trauma, or emotional unpredictability, your system can get stuck in survival mode. It starts reacting to everyday moments like they're emergencies, and connection begins to feel unsafe.

Understanding your nervous system is about more than just knowing how it works. It's about learning how to listen to it, to notice its cues, to soothe it when it's overwhelmed, and to rebuild its sense of safety, one moment at a time. Because real, lasting transformation doesn't just happen in the mind. It happens when the body feels safe enough to stop bracing and start expanding.

By now, you understand that limiting beliefs are not just mental, they're *biological*. They live in the body, encoded through years of patterning and protection. That's the missing piece for so many people on the healing path: the realization that **belief and biology are inseparable**.

Think of it this way: If your limiting beliefs are the script, your nervous system is the stage crew, controlling the lighting, adjusting the sound, and pulling the curtains. It decides what gets revealed and what stays hidden, based not on logic but on what feels safe.

In my work with clients, I often refer to the nervous system as our **internal guidance system**. It's like a GPS for the soul, constantly signaling whether you're aligned with your truth or caught in the loop of an old survival story.

When clients ask me, *"How do I know if I'm stuck in a limiting belief?"* I always tell them, ***"Your body already knows, you just have to pay attention."***

Over the years, I've cultivated what I call a **baseline of calm**, an inner anchor of steadiness that feels like clarity, groundedness, and quiet self-trust. It's not a state of perfection. I still get triggered. I still spiral sometimes. But I now recognize what it feels like to be *home* in myself. And just as clearly, I can feel when I've veered away from that center.

That tightening in my chest? The restless overthinking? The sense of urgency or unease that doesn't match the moment? That's not just anxiety, it's *information*. It's my nervous system whispering: *"Something's off. You've left yourself. You're believing a story that isn't true or avoiding something that needs your presence."*

This is the body's brilliance. It doesn't just reflect your state, it *reveals* your truth. Every shift in breath, every rise in tension, every flicker of dysregulation is part of your **internal guidance system**. And when you learn to listen, you stop asking, *"What's wrong with me?"* Instead, you begin to ask, *"What is this trying to show me?"*

The goal isn't to live without triggers. It's to know your way back home—back to calm, back to truth, back to the baseline of who you are when you're no longer performing, protecting, or proving and just *being*... aligned, aware, and whole. This is mindfulness in action. Awareness embodied. And it doesn't take years of silent retreats or perfect routines to get there. It takes commitment. It takes the willingness to pause, to check in, and to choose alignment over autopilot.

In the *B.E.C.O.M.I.N.G.* journey, one of the most sacred turning points will be in **Part III: Embodiment—Where the Vision Becomes**

You. No matter how clear your vision is, how powerful your mindset becomes, or how deeply you desire change, if your body doesn't feel safe, your transformation will always have a ceiling.

This is where we bring nervous system wisdom into the spotlight. Not as a side note, but as the *foundation*. Because your body isn't just along for the ride, it's the **keeper of your stories, your survival patterns, and your power**. And when you learn to meet it with compassion, listen to its signals, and restore safety from the inside out, you unlock a level of healing that mindset work alone could never achieve.

This step is about more than regulation. It's about **reclaiming your right to feel safe in your own skin**, so that your growth isn't something you force but something that flows. Because when your body feels safe, you don't just change, you transform.

The Body Is the Storykeeper

Let me take you into a chapter of my life that revealed this truth in a way no textbook ever could.

For decades, I battled a food addiction, trapped in a relentless cycle of binging, purging, and body obsession. I used to believe it was all about willpower... or lack of it. I thought if I could just think differently, *I'd finally be free.* But healing had other plans. What I began to uncover was something far deeper and more surprising: **my nervous system had developed a rhythm of its own.** It was as if my body had memorized the pattern—the time of day, the emotional cues, the inner pressure building, until it became unbearable.

I wasn't thinking about food, and I wasn't even hungry, but right around 3:00 PM every day like clockwork my chest would buzz with urgency, and a silent cue would whisper: *"It's time."* I wasn't choosing to binge. I was being *summoned* by a body that had learned how to survive. You see, when I was a teacher, a job I never truly felt good enough in, I spent my days absorbing stress like a sponge. I held space for everyone else while silently questioning my worth. And by the end of the school day, I was exhausted, emotionally, mentally, and energetically. Without realizing it, my nervous system had found its own way to cope. **3:00 PM became my release valve.** It was the moment my body had come to expect relief, not through rest or regulation but through binging. It wasn't about food. It was about escape.

Over time, this became more than a habit. It became *a ritual of survival*, a deeply conditioned loop in my nervous system. So even after I stopped the behaviors, even after the thoughts shifted and the coping strategies changed... **the urge still came.** Because my body hadn't yet gotten the memo. My nervous system was still reading from the old script: "Stress comes in. 3:00 PM. Time to release." That's when I realized that true healing isn't just about changing your mind. It's about updating the body and rewiring the parts of you that still think you're in danger. It's about tending to the places that are still bracing, still reacting, and still waiting for the old ending.

And that kind of healing doesn't happen through force. It happens through compassion, curiosity, and learning to speak the language of your body, one breath, one signal, and one moment at a time. I started asking myself: Where else is my body guiding me toward survival patterns that no longer serve me? Where else is my nervous system protecting me from pain I'm no longer in?

That was the opening. A turning point. Not the end of the struggle but the beginning of real healing. Not through force but through listening. Not through self-discipline but through compassion. It taught me that my body was never the enemy. It was the **messenger**.

The Nervous System and Toxic Relationships

Let me give you another example, one that many of us recognize: the experience of being in a toxic or dysfunctional relationship.

Maybe you were with someone unpredictable, manipulative, or emotionally unavailable. Or maybe they weren't overtly cruel, but they were subtly dismissive, distant, and impossible to reach. Either way, you learned to walk on eggshells. You monitored their moods before speaking. You anticipated their reactions before acting. You silenced your needs. You made yourself small. You became agreeable, invisible, and easy to love not because you were weak but because **your nervous system was doing its job: keeping you safe.**

And then maybe the relationship ended. But the symptoms didn't. You flinch at raised voices. You feel dread when someone texts, *"We need to talk."* You apologize out of habit, even when you've done nothing wrong. That's not weakness. That's your nervous system remembering. That's your body doing what it was trained to do: keep you safe.

These patterns don't dissolve just because the relationship ends. They become encoded, a survival blueprint. And the beliefs that accompany them...

- *"I have to shrink to stay loved."*
- *"Conflict is dangerous."*
- *"My needs are too much."*

...take root in your body, shaping every interaction that follows.

Sometimes trauma isn't what happened *to* you. It's what happened *inside* you in the absence of safety. It's the accumulation of tiny moments when your emotional needs went unmet. When you were too scared to speak. When you had to silence your authenticity to preserve connection.

Before we had language, we had sensation. Before we could explain, we learned to brace.

Our nervous systems became fluent in vigilance long before we knew what anxiety was. Even now, you might not remember the details, but **your body does**. You might feel your throat tighten when you're asked to speak up or your stomach knots at the thought of disappointing someone. You might go numb during conflict or say *"I'm sorry"* on autopilot.

These aren't flaws. They are **survival codes**, the echoes of unspoken stories that were never safe to tell.

Safety Over Success

Here's the hard truth your body has known all along: the nervous system doesn't care about your success, fulfillment, or even your joy. It cares about your *survival.* Which means it will cling to what is familiar, even when that familiarity is filled with dysfunction, disappointment, or emotional scarcity.

Your nervous system would rather you stay in the comfort of the known than risk the perceived danger of the unknown. That's why stepping into a new relationship, speaking your truth, or even resting when you're used to hustle can feel so unsafe. You're not lazy. You're not self-sabotaging. You're responding from a nervous system that's scanning your environment and whispering, *"This is unfamiliar. We don't know if it's safe."*

You can *know* you're worthy. You can *believe* you're ready. And still, your body might slam the brakes. Because to your nervous system, the unknown, joy, abundance, love, visibility, equals *risk.* We call these limiting beliefs. But they're not just thoughts to be changed, they're *protective programs* embedded in the body. And until your body feels safe, your beliefs will fight to return to what it knows.

Let's reframe some things:

- That perfectionism? A hyper-vigilant fight response trying to control your environment to stay safe.
- That burnout? A freeze response that comes when your nervous system collapses under chronic stress.
- That need to over-give? A fawn response rooted in your body's attempt to secure attachment.

You are not flawed. You are brilliantly adapted. But what once protected you may now be holding you back. And healing doesn't mean erasing those patterns. It means teaching your nervous system a new way to feel safe in your truth.

Co-Regulation: We Heal in Connection

You were wounded in relationships, and you will be healed in relationships. Whether it's with a therapist, a coach, a partner, a breathwork circle, or even the quiet presence of nature, *your body learns safety through connection.*

This is why nervous system healing is the missing key in so many self-help journeys. Without it, you're trying to think your way out of patterns that your body still believes are necessary for survival.

So how do you begin? By asking yourself:

- What is my body feeling like in *this* moment?
- Where is the tension?
- What emotion is rising up? fear? shame? anger?
- What is my body trying to protect me from?

Write it out. Let your body tell the story. Because the story isn't just in your mind. It's in your muscles, your breath, your posture, your impulses. And awareness is the beginning of liberation.

You Are Safe to Expand

This chapter isn't about fixing. It's about *rewiring.* You've survived. Now it's time to *thrive.*

Your nervous system is not your enemy. It is your ally. But it needs new data. So give it evidence that it's safe to be seen, safe to rest, safe to say no, safe to feel joy, safe to be powerful, and most of all, safe to be you. Let that safety become your new story.

CHAPTER 6

Mindfulness and Awareness

The Awakening Begins

"You can't stop the waves, but you can learn to surf."

—Jon Kabat-Zinn

Before we explore the formula, we need to lay the foundation. Mindfulness and awareness are where it all begins. They are essential tools that open the door to transformation. Mindfulness and awareness are at the heart of this *becoming* process, and understanding them is key to everything that follows.

That moment is mindfulness. That clarity is awareness.

These aren't trendy concepts or soft suggestions. They are sacred keys, tools to unlock the invisible cage of limiting beliefs that have kept you small, silent, or stuck in toxic relationships. If you've ever felt paralyzed by self-doubt, sabotaged by an inner voice that whispers,

"You're not good enough," or frustrated by the way the same old patterns keep playing out despite your best intentions, then what you're about to discover is nothing short of revolutionary.

This chapter is where your awakening begins, not the kind of awakening filled with fluff and feel-good mantras or surface inspiration dressed up for social media, but the deep, raw, life-altering kind. Because if you want to truly break free, you have to understand what's been keeping you bound. You have to learn how your brain works, how your subconscious stores old programs like a playlist you never meant to hit repeat on. You have to witness the stories you've been telling yourself on autopilot for years.

Mindfulness and awareness are not luxuries; they are lifelines. They are how we stop reacting and start reclaiming and how we interrupt the old programming and finally say, "I see you, but you no longer get to run the show."

This chapter isn't about learning to meditate in a candlelit room (unless that's your vibe). It's about learning to meet yourself in the raw, messy, beautiful moments of your life with presence, curiosity, and compassion. It's about learning to ride the waves of emotion without drowning in them. And most importantly, it's about becoming conscious of the unconscious patterns that have been steering your life from the shadows. Because once you see the pattern, *you can choose differently.*

So let's break this down: **Mindfulness is presence. Awareness is perspective.** One anchors you in the *now*; the other helps you understand the *why.*

Mindfulness is the sacred pause, the act of showing up to the present moment with curiosity and compassion, even when your mind is noisy and your emotions are swirling. It's not about achieving perfect calm or clearing your mind of all thoughts. It's about witnessing what's happening inside you without getting swept away. Mindfulness teaches you to watch the waves without drowning in them.

When you apply mindfulness to limiting beliefs, it becomes your superpower. It allows you to catch the thought before it carries you into a spiral. You get to say, "Oh, there it is again: 'I'm not good enough.' I see it. I recognize it. I don't have to believe it." Mindfulness breaks the trance of automatic thinking. It pulls you out of the story and into the truth of the moment. Then comes awareness, and awareness takes you deeper.

Awareness is the inner lens that lets you explore the internal landscape of your beliefs. It invites you to ask the powerful questions: "*Where did this come from? Why do I believe it? Who gave me this lens through which I view myself and the world? Is this thought really serving me?*" Awareness is what helps you see the threads of old conditioning, how one moment, one comment, one relationship shaped the way you see yourself today.

If mindfulness helps you *observe* the thought, awareness helps you *understand* it. If mindfulness says, "This is a thought," awareness says, "Here's why it's showing up." And when you bring the two together, when you meet the present moment with presence and the past with perspective, you ignite transformation.

Let's say you're in a meeting, and you want to speak up. But suddenly, a wave of anxiety hits, and a familiar inner voice whispers, "You're going to mess this up. They're going to think you're an idiot." Mindfulness helps you pause and notice that voice instead of reacting to it. Awareness helps you trace it back, maybe to a teacher who embarrassed you in class or a parent who only praised perfection. Suddenly, you see it. You feel the pattern. You realize this voice isn't truth. It's a memory.

And in that realization? **You find freedom—freedom to choose.** You step off autopilot and into intention. You stop identifying with your limiting beliefs and begin to question them. You stop obeying the fear and start rewriting the story.

This chapter isn't about becoming someone else. It's about becoming someone *aware*, someone awake to their own thoughts, their own stories, and their own potential. It's about learning to stand in the eye of the storm and say, "*I may feel* fear, but *I am not* fear. I am the one watching it, and I get to choose."

When you master the art of mindfulness and awareness, you don't just break through limiting beliefs. **You become the person who was never truly limited to begin with.**

Mindfulness and awareness are not just practices, they're game-changers. They are the starting point for any real, lasting shift. If you want to stop living by old, unconscious beliefs and start living with clarity and intention, this is where it all begins.

Let's talk about what makes this work so powerful. Your brain is not hardwired for failure. It's not locked into a fixed set of patterns. It's *brilliantly adaptable.* Thanks to **neuroplasticity**, your brain is constantly reshaping itself in response to your experiences and repeated actions. That means every time you bring mindful attention to a limiting belief, every time you interrupt that automatic voice that says, *"You can't,"* or *"You're not enough,"* you're rewiring your brain. Literally. You're forging a new pathway. And over time, that new path becomes stronger, clearer, and more automatic.

Mindfulness also helps quiet the **default mode network**, the part of your brain responsible for looping self-talk, rumination, and fear-based assumptions. When you practice mindfulness, you interrupt those loops. You step out of the storm and into the stillness. You stop being consumed by your thoughts and start observing them. *And from that place of observation, you reclaim your power.*

If limiting beliefs are like an invisible cage, then mindfulness is the flashlight that helps you see the bars, and awareness is the key that unlocks the door.

Now, let me be clear: **traditional meditation absolutely holds value.** I deeply honor and respect the rich wisdom behind seated, contemplative practice. In fact, it's been a vital part of my own healing journey. But what I want you to know is that you don't have to meditate in the traditional sense to experience the benefits of mindfulness. You don't need a quiet room, a cushion, or even 20 uninterrupted minutes (though if that's your thing, that's beautiful). Mindfulness isn't about escaping life. It's about *meeting it more fully*, wherever you are.

It's in the way you breathe before answering that text, the way you notice tension in your shoulders before reacting, and the way you pause and ask, *"Is this fear talking… or truth?"*

These moments are not small. They are **everything**. This is how it starts:

- You catch yourself about to say "yes" when your soul is screaming "no."
- You notice that inner critic trying to narrate your worth, and you turn the volume down.
- You feel the wave of anxiety rise, and instead of drowning in it, you ride it with grace.

Each moment of presence is a *win!* It's a thread pulled from the old fabric of who you thought you had to be. It's not flashy. It's not always comfortable. But it's *profound*. Because each time you show up with mindfulness and awareness, you're choosing freedom over fear. Intention over autopilot. Truth over conditioning.

And if you're wondering where to begin, start here:

The Noticing Practice

Pause just three times a day and ask yourself

- *What am I thinking right now? What story is playing?*
- *What am I feeling in my body?*
- *Is this thought rooted in fear, or in truth?*

You don't have to judge it. You don't have to fix it. Just notice it. Just witness it. Because *awareness alone changes things*. Awareness disrupts the pattern. Mindfulness helps you build a new one. And together? They are your path to becoming.

This chapter isn't just about learning, it's about *awakening*. It's about finally seeing the difference between who you've been taught to be and who you really are.

Theory vs. Practice

Ah yes, it all sounds beautiful in theory, doesn't it? *Just embrace mindfulness and awareness, meditate a little, break free from limiting beliefs, and voilà, life magically transforms.*

But let's get real for a minute. What does this *actually* look like in practice? In real life, mindfulness isn't all soft music and serene mountaintops. Sometimes it looks like sitting down for five minutes to check in with your thoughts only to realize your mind is behaving like an over-caffeinated squirrel with a to-do list. (Fellow ADHDers will totally relate.)

In practice, mindfulness might look like sitting down with the best intentions, only to find your mind bouncing from one unfinished task to the next like a toddler on espresso. Suddenly, everything you've been putting off—laundry, bills, emails, appointments—starts waving at you like it's hosting a reunion in your head. You try to breathe deeply, but instead of finding calm, you're wondering if you're breathing *too deeply* or not deep enough. *"Am I doing this right? Is this normal? Why do I feel light-headed? Is this growth or a panic attack?"*

And then, like clockwork, your inner critic slides in with that familiar smirk: *"Mindfulness? Seriously? We've tried this before, remember? Epic fail. Let's not set ourselves up for disappointment again."* This is the moment most people walk away, believing they're "bad" at mindfulness.

But the truth? **This is the moment the real work begins.**

It's not about being perfect. Mindfulness isn't about making your mind as still as a monk on a mountaintop. It's about showing up for the mental chaos and simply noticing it, without judgment, without trying to wrestle it into submission. Mindfulness was never about silencing your thoughts or achieving some perfect mental stillness. It's about showing up to the noise with compassion. It's about witnessing your inner chaos and choosing to stay present anyway.

You don't need to be calm to be mindful. You don't need to feel peaceful to be present. You just need to be willing to *notice* without judgment.

So maybe your practice today looks like sitting with racing thoughts, tangled emotions, or a restless body. That's not failure. That's being human. And it still counts. Because transformation doesn't happen in one perfect, silent meditation. It happens in the *decision* to return, to show up, again and again, even if you're a little messy, a little distracted, and a little unsure.

It happens in those subtle moments: When you pause before reacting, when you notice yourself about to spiral and gently choose a different response, when you whisper, *"I see you, fear… but you don't get the final say today."* That's where the shift begins. Not with perfection, but with presence.

And remember, this isn't a race. It's a series of tiny, imperfect steps forward, each one inching you closer to a deeper sense of awareness and freedom. So take a deep breath and give yourself some grace. It all sounds great in theory, but in practice? It's about showing up, even if you're showing up as a hot mess. And honestly, that's still progress.

So do it now. Take a breath. Let go of the pressure to "do it right." Give yourself permission to begin exactly where you are, no polished version needed. This journey isn't about mastering mindfulness. It's about remembering yourself.

Mindfulness and Awareness—A Way of Life

When I first dipped my toes into mindfulness and awareness, it wasn't exactly a seamless transition. My ADHD brain, with its browser-hopping intensity and sensory overload, had other plans. My limiting beliefs didn't just dissolve because I'd decided I was ready to grow. And my intrusive thoughts? They didn't quiet down just because I started paying attention. If anything, at first, it all felt louder.

But here's what I learned: That's part of the process. The moment you begin tuning in, you realize just how much noise has been running the show behind the scenes. It's like walking into a cluttered room you've avoided for years. It's overwhelming at first. But then, little by little, you begin sorting through the mess. You don't judge it. You simply witness it. You create space. You breathe.

With time, mindfulness and awareness became more than tools I reached for, they became the lens through which I experienced life. They stopped being something I practiced at set times and instead became how I moved through the world. Conversations became more intentional. Reactions softened into responses. I felt myself pause more and spiral less. I started catching those thought patterns before they caught me. I wasn't perfect, not even close, but I was present. And that was everything.

And let me be honest with you: my life is still miles from perfect. But it has *unrecognizably improved* from what it was before I chose mindfulness and awareness as my way of life. There is less chaos, less drama, and fewer moments where I speak or act out of impulse only to carry regret afterward. There's more clarity now, more calm, and more grace.

I'm not always zen. I still lose my footing at times. But there's an inner peace now, a deeper trust in myself, in my process. I've traded frantic urgency for intention. I've learned to let things breathe and to let *myself* breathe. And even when life throws me off course, I no longer spiral without direction. I know how to come back.

One moment that stands out as a perfect example of this practice in real life happened just after I moved into my new office, what I proudly called my "big girl" space. I was sitting in my chair, taking it all in, feeling proud and grounded, when out of nowhere, I heard it:

"You're never happy with what you have. It's never enough. You always want more than everyone else."

That voice stopped me cold. It was sharp, familiar, and it didn't feel like mine. But in that moment, I recognized it instantly. I could trace it all the way back to a conversation I'd had as a teenager. I remembered the room, the tone, and most of all, the feeling, the sting of shame that came from wanting more than I was "supposed" to want. The unspoken rule that dreaming big was greedy, that desiring more meant you were ungrateful, and that my ambition made others uncomfortable.

The *old* version of me, the one who hadn't yet learned to pause and listen beneath the noise, would have taken that thought as fact. I would have swallowed it whole. Felt the tightening in my chest. The familiar guilt rising. Maybe even shame.

Shame for wanting to upgrade my space.

Shame for wanting *more.*

And because I wouldn't have recognized the belief operating underneath it all, I would have found a way to derail it. Not dramatically. Quietly. A scheduling error. A sudden wave of doubt. A subtle distancing from the very excitement that had once lit me up.

Because when you're still living inside a story that was never truly yours, expansion feels dangerous.

So you stay small.

You make yourself smaller than the life calling you forward.

But this time was different. Because as I sat in *my* chair, in *my* space, and in full awareness, I didn't collapse into that old voice. I smiled. I breathed. And I said, *"I hear you. I recognize you. I know exactly whose story that is, and it's sure as hell not mine. I give it back."*

Then I followed it up with something stronger, something rooted in *my* truth:

"I deserve every inch of this space. I am allowed to want more. I am allowed to dream without limits. I am ambitious, daring, and bold, and I make no apologies for that."

That is the power of awareness and mindfulness working together, not just in theory but in real life, not in a quiet room with incense burning but in the *everyday moments* when an old voice tries to dim your light, and you choose to meet it with love, clarity, and ownership, to speak back with truth.

This is what it looks like when mindfulness and awareness become your way of life. You stop operating from survival mode and start living with intention. You stop reacting from old wounds and start responding from grounded wisdom. You stop chasing perfection and start honoring your progress.

And sure, I'm still a work in progress. But I like who I'm becoming. And more importantly, I *know* who I'm becoming. That's the quiet power of this path. It doesn't always shout. It doesn't need to. It simply reminds you, again and again:

You are here. You are aware. And you are becoming.

CHAPTER 7

B.E.C.O.M.I.N.G.

A Method, A Movement, A Formula

> "Your life does not get better by chance; it gets better by change."
>
> —Jim Rohn

There is a sacred moment in every transformation, a point where clarity meets courage, and the desire for change becomes a decision. It's that moment when something inside you whispers, "*This is it.*" Not someday. Not when you're more prepared, more healed, more "ready." Now.

You've done the inner excavation. You've started peeling back the layers, revealing the quiet beliefs that have quietly dictated your story for far too long. And now, here you are, at the edge of a new identity, a new reality, a new way of being.

This isn't just a chapter. It's your crossroads where clarity collides with courage, where healing demands action, where your *becoming* is no longer a hope; it's a choice. And let me be clear: **Inspiration may open the door, but only action will carry you across the threshold.**

We live in a world addicted to *preparation*, to consuming the wisdom of others while quietly doubting our own. But readiness doesn't arrive on a silver platter. It's summoned by your willingness to move, even if your voice shakes and your feet are unsure.

You don't need more time. You need a moment of truth. And this is it. Because real change? It doesn't live in your mind. It lives in your movement. It lives in the uncomfortable conversations, the brave boundaries, the rewritten beliefs, and the daring steps toward the life your soul has always known was meant for you.

This is the shift from knowing to doing, from insight to implementation, from reflection to realignment. And I know what you may be wondering: *Is there really a way through this, a path, an actual path to wellness? Or is transformation just something the lucky few stumble into?* I used to wonder the same thing. Until I lived it. I've lived the question of whether things can change. And I've lived the answer. And let me tell you, it's yes. Hell yes.

I confidently claim this truth not because I've read all the books (though I've devoured my share), and not because I've studied psychology or human behavior from a safe academic distance, but because *I've lived it*—not in a perfect, polished way but in the raw, unfiltered trenches of real life, through addiction, anxiety, grief, burnout, people-pleasing, and painful awakenings that stripped me bare. I've known the heartbreak of losing myself in the name of being "enough." I also know the power in reclaiming what was mine all along, my voice, my worth, my *truth*.

After the events of 2023 shook me to my core and stripped away everything but the truth, something undeniable clicked: what I had been doing to heal and expand wasn't just working, it was transformational. And it wasn't luck. It wasn't a fluke. It was *real*. It was *repeatable*. And, most importantly, it was *teachable*.

So I did what I've always done when life calls me deeper. I listened, I reflected, and I got radically honest. I combed through my own journey, tracing the thread through every rise and every fall. I revisited the breakthroughs and the breaking points. And in that process, I began to see it, *a pattern*, not just in my story but in the stories of my clients, too. I saw people releasing decades of self-doubt, walking away from cycles that once defined them, and stepping boldly into the lives they were always meant to lead. These weren't isolated wins. These were awakenings, systematic, sustainable, and soul-deep.

That's when it hit me: there was a method behind the process, a rhythm to the rise. There was a *formula*. What I uncovered wasn't some feel-good theory or fleeting insight. It was a set of guiding principles, timeless, grounded, and deeply practical, that formed the foundation of every lasting transformation I'd ever witnessed, including my own.

It became so clear to me. And once I saw it, a blueprint for real change, I couldn't unsee it. So I rolled up my sleeves. I went to work. I tested it. I tweaked it. And I refined it, again and again, until what remained was something I could stand behind with every fiber of my being.

And now, it's in your hands.

B.E.C.O.M.I.N.G.

It's an 8-step, soul-led formula designed to free you from the mental traps, emotional loops, and inherited stories that have kept you playing small. It's a proven roadmap to help you reclaim your power, rewrite your narrative, and live the life your higher self has been trying to lead you to all along.

If this book has found its way to you, it's because something inside you already knows it's time. It's time to stop shrinking to fit into places you've long outgrown. It's time to stop hoping change will find you and instead *become* the change you've been waiting for.

This isn't just a roadmap. It's a revolution. It's a loud defiance of every belief that ever told you "not yet," "not enough," or "not for you." It's a return to what's always been true beneath your doubt, your strength, your worth, and your voice. It's a steady reclaiming of your power, your path, and the permission to live as the fullest version of yourself, not in theory, not in whispers, but in action.

Let's stop waiting for the perfect moment and become the moment. Let's embody the transformation we've been craving, one choice, one breath, one brave step at a time.

Let's rise with intention, with power, and with no turning back.

B.E.C.O.M.I.N.G.: A Fusion of What Works—Science, Soul, and Strategy

If you're anything like me, you've probably seen a lot of "transformational" programs before. And maybe you're wondering, *"How is this any different? How do I know this isn't just another feel-good formula wrapped in fancy words?"*

I get it. The skepticism is valid. Because when you've tried to change before and ended up back in the same place, you start to wonder if *anything* truly works. So let me reassure you right now: this is not another surface-level mindset hack. This is a formula that works because it's rooted in evidence, experience, and real, lasting transformation.

The formula is a fusion of the most powerful, proven approaches in modern psychology, neuroscience, and behavior change, woven together with soul, compassion, and intention. It's not just here to help you think differently for a moment. It's here to help you live differently for a lifetime, to rewire your beliefs, your habits, and your emotional patterns at the deepest level.

Let's break it down.

At its core is Cognitive Behavioral Therapy (CBT)—a transformative tool for identifying and challenging the limiting beliefs that have been shaping your life. CBT helps you become aware of your inner dialogue and teaches you how to reframe those negative thought loops that hold you back. This is where you begin to realize that the story you've been telling yourself isn't the only story available to you.

From there, we add the heart-opening wisdom of Mindfulness-Based Cognitive Therapy (MBCT) because real change doesn't begin with more effort. It begins with more awareness. MBCT teaches you how to witness your thoughts without becoming them. It creates space between the moment something happens and how you choose to respond. This is essential in the "Noticing Patterns" and "Defining Your Vision" stages, where clarity, calm, and conscious reflection become your compass.

Awareness is where transformation is born. And neuroscience backs this up. Research shows that simply by observing a thought or habit with non-judgmental awareness, you begin to loosen its grip. Why? Because what you witness, you can rewire.

Next, we draw on Dialectical Behavior Therapy (DBT), a compassionate approach that helps you build emotional strength and resilience. DBT teaches you to feel deeply without being overwhelmed, to sit with discomfort without losing yourself, and to hold space for both acceptance and change. This is your lifeline when old emotions like shame, fear, or grief rise to the surface during the healing process.

We also integrate the wisdom of Acceptance and Commitment Therapy (ACT), which offers one of the most liberating truths you'll ever hear: You don't have to eliminate every negative thought or emotion to move forward. You simply have to stop letting them drive your life. ACT gives you the tools to take aligned action even when it's uncomfortable, which is an essential part of the "Transformation Through Resolve" step in this journey.

And then there's habit change science, a vital piece of the puzzle that's often overlooked. According to experts like James Clear (author of *Atomic Habits*) and neuroscientists like Dr. Judson Brewer, real change doesn't come from willpower alone. It comes from interrupting the habit loop, rewiring your identity, and practicing new behaviors with consistency and intention. That's why this formula includes daily micro-practices and identity shifts, because transformation doesn't happen in one big moment. It happens in the tiny, brave choices you make every single day.

And here's where something truly powerful comes in: neuro-association. Rooted in the early work of Ivan Pavlov and developed through decades of psychological and neuroscientific research, neuro-association explains how your brain creates emotional links between experiences. Over time, we start to associate failure with pain, success with pleasure, or visibility with vulnerability and rejection. These subconscious connections become the emotional architecture of our lives, until we decide to rewrite them.

In this process, you'll learn how to use neuro-association to your advantage, to link growth with safety, discipline with freedom, action with empowerment. You'll learn how to reshape the meaning your brain attaches to change, so transformation becomes not only possible but sustainable.

The formula also honors the strengths-based approaches of Solution-Focused Therapy and Positive Psychology. These frameworks don't ask, "What's wrong with you?" They ask, "What's already strong in you?" They help you reconnect with your resilience, remember your wins, and build forward from hope, not fear.

So what does all of this mean for you? It means this isn't just about thinking better thoughts. It's about becoming a truer version of yourself, not by becoming someone else but by coming home to who you really are. You're not just breaking patterns. You're building a new identity. You're rewiring your brain, your beliefs, and your future, step by step, from the inside out.

And if there's a small voice inside still whispering, *"Can I really do this?"* Let me tell you with everything I have: Yes, you can. You wouldn't be here if you weren't ready. You don't need perfection. You just need willingness.

Here's the thing, this isn't just a method. It's a mirror, a map, and a movement. It's here to remind you of your power and walk you back to your truth. So take a deep breath. Trust the process. And let's walk this path together, one powerful, conscious, soul-led step at a time.

Anchoring Your Insight: Practical Tools for Lasting Change

Awareness is powerful, but it's what you *do* with that awareness that changes your life. Insight alone is not enough. Transformation asks for more. It asks you to show up, to apply, to embody. That's why the B.E.C.O.M.I.N.G. Method isn't just about understanding the mechanics of change, it's about *living* it.

For every step in this formula, you'll find practical tools and exercises, carefully designed to meet you exactly where you are, whether you're just waking up to your patterns or deep in the work of personal evolution. These are more than exercises. They're invitations, gateways, each one a stepping stone toward the version of you that's been waiting on the other side of fear, habit, or hesitation.

Let's be honest, change doesn't happen through osmosis. You can't just read about growth and expect your life to shift. Insight without implementation is potential left on the table. But when you *engage*, when you put pen to page, challenge old beliefs, and take aligned action, something powerful clicks. You move from knowing to *becoming*, from hoping to doing. **You can access the full B.E.C.O.M.I.N.G. Workbook—at becomingnow.ca.**

It's your guided space to do the work, unlock the breakthroughs, and step into who you were always meant to be.

And here's the beautiful part: this isn't just mindset work, it's neuroscience. Your brain *rewires* through repetition. Every time you interrupt a limiting belief and choose a different response, you're literally carving a new neural pathway. What once felt impossible begins to feel familiar. Empowered. Natural. You're not just changing your thoughts, you're changing your *internal architecture*. You're teaching your nervous system how to feel safe while expanding.

At the end of each chapter, you'll find a space called **The Takeaway**, a reflection practice inspired by the same powerful awareness exercise I use with clients at the end of every session.

This is your moment to pause and witness your own evolution, to acknowledge that you are no longer the same person who began this chapter. Something within you has shifted, subtly, profoundly, and undeniably.

With each insight, your awareness has expanded. With each truth, another layer of limitation has been lifted. With each page, you're remembering who you truly are, not who you were told to be.

This is where transformation takes root, in your willingness to notice how far you've already come. Why? Because transformation doesn't just come from what you read, it comes from what you *claim.* By taking the time to write it down, you're training your mind to recognize growth, to integrate new truths, and to stay open to the possibilities ahead.

This simple act of reflection isn't small; it's foundational. It's how you begin rewiring your inner narrative, one breakthrough at a time. And this moment right here? It's the first of many on your journey from awareness to embodiment. This isn't about racing through the work to reach the finish line. It's about creating the kind of slow, steady, soul-led shift that sticks. It's about being present in your awareness, your rituals, your honest reflections.

So as we move forward, remember: **Growth isn't a one-time leap. It's a daily choice.** It's not about perfection. It's about presence. Not speed, but *devotion.* Because this isn't just a book you read. It's a path you walk, a truth you reclaim, and a *becoming* you live into, one page, one breath, one choice at a time. This is the part where things start to accelerate. This is where insight becomes momentum. This is where you go from *thinking about change* to *becoming the change.*

So listen closely. You are *not* the exception. You are *not* the one person out of 9 billion or so who is destined to stay stuck, who doesn't get to heal, who isn't capable of transformation. That belief? That's just another lie your mind has been conditioned to tell you. You are *not* different from me in some impossible way. I don't have superpowers. I wasn't handed some magical ability to break free while you were left behind. The only thing that separates where I was from where I am now is a choice, the choice to do the work, to challenge the old stories, and to believe, even when it felt impossible, that something *more* was waiting for me. And let me be clear: *more is possible for you, too.*

If I can shatter the chains of my limiting beliefs, rewrite my story, and step into a life I once thought was out of reach, then so can you. *You are capable. You are worthy. You are powerful beyond measure.* And I am here to walk this path with you.

You don't need to have all the answers. You don't need to be fearless or have it all figured out. You just need to be *willing* to take the first step. So, are you ready? Because on the other side of this process is *you*, the real you, the limitless you, the you who is no longer defined by old stories and self-imposed limitations.

As I've mentioned in the introduction, the ideas, tools, and approaches you'll encounter on this path to transformation are not entirely original to me. Some of these principles are timeless, tested by countless others over generations.

What I was able to do? I've done the messy work of trial and error, picked out the right ingredients, and arranged them into a formula that actually works. It's like baking a masterpiece: the magic isn't in each individual ingredient but in how they all come together to create something amazing. That's exactly what this formula is: a well-crafted recipe for transformation that has the potential to change your life.

So let me be clear, crystal clear: I'm not just offering you a process. I'm offering you a path that's been walked. Tested. Proven. And I'm walking it with you. I am here because this work saved me. I can guide you because I *am* the evidence that this works.

Now for the moment you've been waiting for... let's get to it!

The Formula

I know you're itching to dive headfirst into the formula, and trust me, I *love* that energy! Let's set you up for success with a few essential insights to help you *get the most* out of this journey. So hang tight, because you are *this close* to a breakthrough that could change everything.

First, take a moment to acknowledge something powerful: *You're here.* You made it this far, and that is no small thing. It means you've already started dismantling the belief that you're stuck, that change isn't possible for you, or that you don't deserve transformation. Some part of you, no matter how small, *already believes* in something more.

And that's everything.

Transformation doesn't start with the final breakthrough moment, it starts *here*, in the quiet decision to keep going. In the simple but powerful act of turning the page, leaning in, and saying *yes* to yourself.

So before we go any further, *celebrate this*. Seriously. Do a happy dance, fist pump the air, or just close your eyes and soak in this moment. Because whether you realize it or not, you've already started the work. And trust me, this is just the beginning.

Now, let's dive in.

Preparing for Your Transformation: Essential Tips

Let's set the stage for your success. Think of this as gathering your tools before starting a masterpiece. You wouldn't build a house without a solid foundation, right? The same applies here. This process is designed to create lasting change, but it requires commitment, presence, and a willingness to lean in.

Here are your essential guidelines to get the most out of this journey:

Tip #1: Transformation is cumulative—no skipping ahead!

Each step of this formula builds on the last, creating a solid foundation for real, lasting transformation. This isn't a quick-fix approach where you cherry-pick the easy parts and skip the deeper work. Trust the process. Move forward *only* when you've fully engaged with each step. There's no rush. Healing and growth happen in their own time. This is your journey, not a race.

Tip #2: Have a journal or writing materials handy.

You'll be uncovering powerful insights along the way, and trust me, you *will* want to write them down. Your journal will become a mirror reflecting your growth, a roadmap of your breakthroughs, and a testimony to the work you've done. I personally carry a journal everywhere, not because I write in it every day, but because I know that when inspiration strikes, I'll want to capture it.

Tip #3: Stock up on sticky notes.

Seriously. Sticky notes will become your best friend. Use them to jot down affirmations, reminders, or "a-ha" moments. Stick them on your bathroom mirror, your laptop, your fridge, anywhere you'll see them often. Let them serve as gentle nudges to stay on track.

Tip #4: Clean your mirror—literally.
Yes, you read that right! Grab some window cleaner and make that mirror shine because you're going to be using it for some powerful mirror work. This isn't just about reflection, it's about seeing yourself clearly, with compassion and honesty.

Tip #5: Find your quiet space.
Identify a place where you can be alone, even if it's just for five minutes a day. It can be a peaceful corner of your home, your car, your office, wherever you can take a breath and tune in. And if that place happens to be your bathroom? No judgment here! Some of my best revelations have come while sitting on the bathroom floor.

Tip #6: Don't take yourself too seriously.
Transformation isn't just about deep introspection, it's about joy, play, and discovery. You'll be singing, dancing, and stepping out of your comfort zone. Expect to feel silly at times. That's a *good* thing!

Tip #7: Most importantly, have fun with this!
This is *your* journey. Let it be messy, magical, and uniquely yours. Celebrate the small wins, embrace the unexpected moments, and remember, this isn't about perfection. It's about progress.

You're officially ready to kick things off! I can't even tell you how excited I am for you, let's get this transformation show on the road!

CHAPTER 8

B.E.C.O.M.I.N.G.

The Formula That Changes Everything

> "Healing isn't becoming someone else, it's unbecoming everything you're not."
>
> –Monic Ayotte

The **B.E.C.O.M.I.N.G. Formula** is more than a sequence of steps. It's a journey. And like every true journey of transformation, it unfolds in **phases**.

As you move through this process, you'll notice that each step builds on the one before it. That's intentional. Because healing doesn't happen all at once. It happens in layers. It happens in rhythm. It happens through *integration*.

That's why I've broken this formula into **three powerful phases**:

- **Awakening**—where you shine light on what's been running you
- **Activation**—where you begin to imagine
  and embody what's possible
- **Embodiment**—where the change becomes who you are

This structure gives you clarity, momentum, and a deeper sense of purpose at every stage of your becoming. So as you move forward, know this:

You're not just learning a formula. You're moving through the natural arc of your own becoming, from awareness, to vision, to embodiment. And by the end of this journey, you won't just *understand* the shift. *You'll be living it.*

This isn't just about healing. It's not just about productivity or goals or positive thinking. It's about **who you are becoming.** Because real transformation, the kind that lasts, that liberates, that roots itself in your bones, doesn't happen in your head alone. It's not just insight. It's **integration**. It's not just mindset. It's **embodiment**. It's not about fixing who you are. It's about **remembering who you were before the world taught you to shrink**.

That's why I created *The B.E.C.O.M.I.N.G. Formula*, a method designed to walk you, step by step, out of old patterns and into a new life experience, not through pressure but through presence, not through hustle but through healing. You don't just need better habits. You need a new home inside yourself, one built on safety, self-trust, and ownership.

This formula doesn't ask you to leap into someone else's version of "better." It invites you to return to the most grounded, powerful, aligned version of you, the one who already exists beneath the fear, the perfectionism, the people-pleasing, the protective coping.

Each letter in B.E.C.O.M.I.N.G. represents a step in that unfolding where you'll experience:

- A shift in awareness
- A rewiring of the nervous system
- A claiming of self-worth
- A shedding of stories
- A redefinition of your identity
- A commitment to intentional action

- And a life that finally *feels* like yours

This isn't about dipping your toes in. This is about **stepping in fully**, soul-first. You didn't come this far to stay the same. You came to **rise**.

So take a breath, not because you're bracing but because you're finally ready to *own it*. This is your moment. Your permission. No more shrinking. No more waiting. Let this be the moment you stop seeking and start ***becoming***.

Let's do this!

B.E.C.O.M.I.N.G.

The 8-Step Formula to Break Through Limiting Beliefs and Become Who You Were Always Meant to Be

Part I—Awakening: See the Pattern, Break the Spell

This is the foundational work: awareness, ownership, and emotional truth-telling. This is where you wake up from unconscious beliefs and begin to reclaim your power:

B – Break the Spell of Old Beliefs

Spot the unconscious narrative

E – Embrace Accountability

Own your part without shame or blame

C – Challenge the Conditioning

Trace the roots and question what's been running the show

B.E.C.O.M.I.N.G.

Break the Spell: Beginning with Awareness

This is where your becoming begins, not with doing, not with fixing, but with *seeing*, using unfiltered, courageous awareness.

The first step on your transformation journey is taking a deep, honest inventory of your life. This means confronting what's truly working and, just as importantly, what isn't. It's about looking at the areas of your life that bring you joy, fulfillment, and peace and at those that cause stress, emotional pain, and dissatisfaction. This self-assessment will give you the clarity you need to see where you're aligned with your true self and where change is calling you. It's the foundation for creating a life that reflects your values, your passions, and your true aspirations. This is the starting point for meaningful, lasting change.

Look around your life. What feels expansive, alive, true? And what feels heavy, tight, unspoken? What have you been tolerating in the name of being fine?

This step isn't about judgment; it's about *truth*. And truth is the most loving force there is. Because when you get real with yourself, when you finally stop pretending, hiding, and minimizing, you create the only condition that transformation requires: honesty. Because awareness isn't passive. It's electric. It's disruptive. It breaks the trance. And once you see clearly, you can't unsee. You realize: *This is my life. And I get to decide what stays, what goes, and what gets rewritten.*

This is the first spark of becoming, not a single moment, but a profound shift in how you see yourself. No more autopilot. No more waiting. Just you, awake to what's real and what awaits transformation.

B.E.C.O.M.I.N.G.

Embrace Accountability: Taking Ownership

> "You are not the story that hurt you. You are the author of what comes next."
>
> — Monic Ayotte

Awareness without responsibility is just observation. This is the moment you move from insight into ownership. You stop pointing fingers at your past, your pain, your programming, and gently, powerfully, take your life back into your own hands. You didn't choose the conditioning. But you do get to choose whether it continues to run your life. Embracing responsibility isn't about guilt or self-blame. It's about power. It's about realizing no one's coming to rescue you, and also, that no one *needs* to. You hold the pen now. This is where you stop waiting. Stop waiting for an apology, for perfect timing, for permission. Choose to participate fully in your healing and your future.

It's not always easy. There's grief here but there is also grace and compassion. Owning your story also means seeing where you stayed small or silent. But that's part of the reclamation. That's how you rise.

You are your own turning point now.

B.E.C.O.M.I.N.G.

Challenge the Conditioning: From Pattern to Possibility

> "You can't release what you're still resisting.
> Healing starts where honesty meets compassion."
>
> — Monic Ayotte

This is where we begin to **challenge the conditioning,** the automatic patterns you didn't choose but have been living by for years, not to relive the past but to finally understand what's been quietly running the show. This is where the unconscious becomes conscious, where the invisible script becomes visible.

In this step, you begin connecting the dots between your current struggles and the beliefs, behaviors, and protective strategies you picked up along the way. You start asking, "*Where did this story begin? Who handed me this role? Why have I been playing it on repeat, even when it no longer fits?*"

You trace the thread back to the origin, not to blame but to reclaim. You begin to see your inner critic, not as a bully but as a younger part of you that learned to stay small to stay safe.

The perfectionism. The control. The overgiving. They all made sense once. But now, they're keeping you stuck. **This is the moment pattern meets possibility.** Because when you name the root, you stop fighting the symptoms. You start to recognize the beliefs buried under your reactions:

"I have to earn love."

"I'm only safe if I'm in control."

"If I fail, I'll be abandoned."

And suddenly, the struggle softens. Your triggers make sense. Your sabotage has context. Your shame has a source. And now, *you have a choice.* Because the moment you **challenge the conditioning**, you begin to open the door from old patterns to new possibilities.

Part II—Activation: Step Into the Vision

This is where you stop looping in thought and start anchoring into feeling. Where belief is no longer just a mindset, it becomes your **felt experience.**

This is where the vision takes root. The bridge between clarity and action.

O – Own the New Vision

Define the self you're becoming

M – Meet Your Becoming

Create safety through embodiment and nervous system alignment

B.E.C.O.M.I.N.G.

Own The New Vision: Where Vision Becomes Blueprint

> "You cannot become who you're meant to be
> while clinging to who you were taught to be."
>
> — Monic Ayotte

After you've faced the truth and connected to the root, this is the moment you look forward with eyes wide open and heart cracked open. This is where you begin to imagine a life beyond the patterns. Beyond the roles. Beyond the old story.

In this step, you stop defining yourself by what you've survived and start dreaming from a place of who you're becoming. You ask yourself, maybe for the first time:

What do I actually want? What would it feel like to build a life based on alignment, not approval? What does my freedom look like? Sound like? Breathe like?

Opening to a new vision isn't about fantasy, it's about *permission*—permission to want what you want, permission to rewrite the narrative, and permission to take up space in your own story. This is where you dare to imagine a version of yourself who's not stuck in survival mode, a version who sets boundaries without guilt, speaks with clarity, and walks with grounded confidence, not because she's perfect but because she finally knows her worth. And here's the beautiful thing: that version of you already exists. She's not far away. She's just buried beneath the conditioning. This step is about calling her forward.

You're no longer designing a life from fear, from rules, from other people's expectations. You're designing it from vision, from truth, from desire. Because the future doesn't just happen, it gets *created.*

And this is where you start.

B.E.C.O.M.I.N.G.
Meet Your Becoming

> "The privilege of a lifetime is to become who you truly are."
>
> — Carl Jung

You've created the vision. You've imagined what life could look like without the old scripts, the protective patterns, and the beliefs that kept you stuck. Now it's time to do the one thing that actually turns vision into reality: embody it.

Here, embodiment becomes the bridge. You're not just thinking new thoughts or making better choices. You're practicing being the version of you who already lives the vision, the one who breathes like she belongs, who walks like she trusts herself, who speaks like she knows she's worthy.

This is the moment when transformation stops being conceptual and becomes cellular. Because once your body believes it, your life begins to reflect it. This is the step where you stop *holding* the vision and start *living* it, not just in your thoughts, but in your breath, your posture, your voice, your choices. Because limiting beliefs don't just live in the mind. They are held in the body. They are encoded in your nervous system, your internal guidance system.

You might believe you're ready. You might feel inspired, clear, and motivated. But if your nervous system still perceives change as a threat, it will quietly pull you back into the familiar, into self-sabotage, procrastination, shrinking, or over-controlling.

This step is about learning to move *with* your nervous system, not against it. You've got to recognize your body's cues, those subtle signals that whisper, "this doesn't feel safe." And instead of overriding them or pushing through, you meet them with presence, compassion, and curiosity. Because your nervous system isn't the problem. It's your guide. It's not broken. It's brilliant. It has always been working for you, not against you, sending signals to protect you, and drawing your attention to where healing is needed most. When you begin to understand its language, tightness, hesitation, and overwhelm, you stop seeing your reactions as resistance and start seeing them as a request for focused attention.

This is where regulation becomes your superpower, not to force change but to **create the internal safety required for your new identity to take root**.

Part III: Embodiment—Where the Vision Becomes You

Becoming doesn't end when the vision is clear. That's where the real work begins.

These final three steps are about *mastery*. Because insight without integration? Fades. Progress without presence? Collapses. And identity without grounding? Cracks under pressure.

I – Integrate with Intention

Bring your awareness into daily practice.

N – Nurture Your Becoming

Hold space for your growth with compassion.

G – *Ground in Your Identity*

Embody the Truth You've Claimed

B.E.C.O.M.I.N.G.

Integrate with Intention: Where Insight Becomes Identity

"To know and not to do is not to know."

— Zen Proverb

Where insight becomes identity through lived practice.

This is the moment where transformation begins to settle, not in your thoughts but in your choices, your rhythms, your nervous system, your life. You've done the work. You've named the belief, softened the fear, and released the survival response. You've seen the vision of who you're becoming, and now it's time to *live her.*

This step is where most people stop. They get the clarity. They feel the breakthrough. But they don't stay with it long enough to make it real.

Integration is the part that matters most because it's where healing becomes a habit. It's where the belief gets practiced until it becomes embodied. It's where your nervous system starts to trust that the threat has passed… and that the new self is safe to emerge.

This step isn't about perfection. It's about *presence.* It's about showing up in real time, in real life, and choosing from the version of you that you're becoming, not just when it's easy but especially when it's not. You begin to:

- Honor boundaries instead of just talking about them.
- Move with self-worth instead of just performing it.
- Breathe through the discomfort of growth instead of retreat from it.

You start becoming someone who doesn't just know what she deserves—**she walks in it.** This is the part where your nervous system experiences consistency and your patterns begin to rewire themselves through practice, not pressure.

It's not glamorous.

It's not loud.

But it's *everything.*

Because this is where the work leaves the page and enters your posture, your pace, your voice, your timing, and your choices. You're no longer chasing her. You're inhabiting her. And with each conscious choice and each embodied moment, **you become less of who you were... and more of who you came here to be.**

B.E.C.O.M.I.N.G.

Nurture Your Becoming

> "Momentum doesn't mean you never slow down.
> It means you know how to rise again, wiser,
> softer, stronger."
>
> — Monic Ayotte

This is the step where you learn to stay with yourself, not just when it's exciting but when it's uncomfortable, when the high wears off, when the path gets quiet, when the old patterns come knocking. Because becoming isn't linear. It's layered. You will rise. You will stall. You will fall back into habits you swore you'd outgrown. And none of that means you're broken. It means you're *becoming.*

This step is about reclaiming momentum, not from force or pressure but from devotion, from the part of you that knows that this isn't about perfection. It's about *presence.* It's about tending to your growth like you would to a fire: consistently, patiently, and without panic when the flames flicker. You learn that growth is not erased by a setback. It's strengthened by how you rise from it.

You create practices that restore your energy instead of draining it. You ask: "*What brings me back to myself? What helps me remember who I'm becoming when I forget?*" You build a relationship with your future self and show up for her, even on the days when progress feels invisible. Because the difference between those who transform and those who don't? It isn't willpower. It's the ability to *reclaim the moment,* to return and to begin again, without shame or judgement.

You let this step be messy. Gentle. Real. You forgive the slip. You celebrate the return. You honor the rhythm of your growth. And in doing so, you become unshakable, not because you never fall but because you *always come back.*

This is the ***Momentum Reclaim***. This is how your *becoming* stays alive.

B.E.C.O.M.I.N.G.
Ground in Your Identity

> "This is where change stops being something you practice and becomes who you are."
>
> — Monic Ayotte

This is the step where you stop reaching and start *rooting.* It just fits.

You've already practiced new beliefs. You've taken action. You've adjusted, reflected, and nurtured your growth. But grounding? Grounding is where it all clicks into place. This is where you *stabilize* the identity you've been building, energetically, emotionally, and subconsciously. You are no longer trying. You are being. You're no longer rehearsing this version of you. You're *embodied* in her. She's how you speak, how you respond, how you walk into a room, how you rest, how you rise, how you lead.

And the power of this moment is that you're no longer surprised by your alignment. You *expect* it. You don't need reminders of your worth. You radiate it. And now? You *are* her.

This is where the shift becomes stable, not a moment of motivation but a new baseline. This is where success feels embodied, softness feels strong, and power feels like it belongs to you, not as a performance but as your truth. Your nervous system recognizes familiar as safety. Your boundaries aren't battles; they're natural. Your worth doesn't need to be proven; it's present.

In this step, your identity becomes *anchored.* Not performative. Not conditional. Not one foot in the old and one in the new. This is no longer about becoming. It's about *being.*

Fully rooted. Fully alive. Fully *you.*

CHAPTER 9

B.E.C.O.M.I.N.G.

Break the Spell, Beginning with Awareness

> "Owning our story can be hard but not nearly as difficult as spending our lives running from it."
>
> — Brené Brown

This is the moment you stop performing and start getting real, not in the filtered, curated, camera-ready kind of way and not the version of your life you post on Facebook, Instagram, TikTok, or anywhere else people only see the highlight reel. You know that version: The smiling vacation selfie with your partner right after a fight, the "grateful for it all" post while quietly drowning in anxiety, or the picture-perfect update that hides how exhausted, overwhelmed, or disconnected you actually feel.

In this step, we're not editing the truth. We're naming it. Because transformation doesn't begin in your public persona. It begins in the places you've kept hidden, even from yourself. This is the step where you get honest about the parts of your life you wouldn't post online while still allowing yourself to celebrate the ones you would.

It's not either/or. It's *both/and.*

You get to honor the things you're proud of. And you get to tell the truth about what's quietly hurting. Because before you can change your life, you have to stop performing it. You have to stop living a version of yourself that only exists to appear "okay."

Awareness starts with this brave act: Looking at the whole picture, not just what you'd openly share but what's playing out behind the screen. Because before you can shift anything, you have to see it. All of it.

This is the work of awareness. You take a breath and pause long enough to actually assess your life, piece by piece, area by area. Your relationships. Your job. Your finances. Your health. Your environment. Your habits. Your daily routines. This is the step where you take inventory, not just of what you do but of what you feel in every corner of your life. You ask yourself:

- What's working here? What energizes me, fulfills me, and makes me proud?
- What's draining me, frustrating me, or quietly eating away at my peace?
- What am I just "putting up with" out of habit or fear?
- What areas of my life have I been avoiding because I don't want to face the truth?

This is not a punishment. This is not about shame. This is about truth-telling. It's about calling a spade a spade and naming what's not working so you can stop pretending that it is. Because anything you refuse to look at will continue to run your life by default. This is where you name the tension in your relationship that you've been pretending isn't there, the job that slowly crushes your soul but pays the bills, the body signals you keep ignoring, the financial stress you've normalized, and the boundaries you keep abandoning in the name of being "nice." This is the step where you see it all. And you name it all.

This is where the illusion breaks and your ***becoming*** begins.

Awareness doesn't mean you fix it all at once. It means you stop hiding from it. It means you meet your life exactly where it is, so you can begin to choose where it's going. This is your truth-telling moment, not because you're broken but because you're done pretending that being "fine" is good enough. The life you want? The peace you crave? The next version of you that's waiting to rise? It all starts here. With awareness. With honesty. With the courage to stop glossing over what hurts and finally face it.

This is the foundation. The clearing. The beginning. And it's yours now. But here's something you should know: this part of the process? It can be challenging, not because it's complicated but because it requires something we rarely give ourselves: *an honest, loving look at the full picture.*

Some people, when they first sit down to do this inventory, can't see clearly. It's not because they're weak. It's not because they're unwilling. But because they've been stuck in dissatisfaction, burnout, or emotional survival mode for *so long* that they've forgotten what joy even looks like. They can't see the forest because they've been trying to survive among the trees. And when that happens, something sneaky shows up: **blanket statements** and **absolute thinking.**

These are the mental filters that flatten your life into a single story, usually one of powerlessness, stuckness, or failure. They sound like:

- *"I'm always depressed."*
- *"Nothing ever changes for me."*
- *"I've just never been a motivated person."*
- *"This is who I am. I've always been this way."*
- *"I'm too broken to fix."*

But here's the thing: these statements aren't the truth. They're **defense mechanisms** your mind built to simplify pain. Because it's easier to say *"I'm just a failure"* than to sit with the heartbreak of trying so hard for so long and still feeling stuck. It's easier to believe *"I'm just not good at relationships"* than to admit how deeply you've been hurt.

Blanket statements protect you from having to feel the full weight of your story. **Absolute thinking** makes it seem like the discomfort you're in now is the only thing you'll ever know.

But these mental shortcuts *will* block you from seeing what's actually going on beneath the surface. And in this step, awareness, you need to be willing to look underneath them. So if you notice yourself saying things like *"everything is a mess"* or *"I'm always exhausted,"* pause. Challenge yourself to go deeper:

- What *specifically* feels like a mess?
- Where am I actually coping better than I give myself credit for?
- What areas *might* be working, even a little?

You don't need to have it all figured out. You just need to stay curious. You need to *keep looking.* Because awareness is a skill to be developed and practiced. And if you've been emotionally overwhelmed, dissociated, or checked out for a while? You might not be able to access the full inventory right away, and that's okay.

The key is to *keep asking* questions. Keep digging. Keep watching for those all-or-nothing thoughts, and instead of accepting them as truth, treat them as red flags and invitations to slow down, get specific, and get honest. If you can do that? You can find your way through the fog. And that's where everything begins to change.

Absolute Thinking: The Illusion of Always or Never

Absolute thinking is when we look at life through a lens of extremes, either it's all good or all bad, with no in-between. It's that "black-and-white" mindset that makes us think in rigid categories: *everything is a failure* or *nothing is ever enough*. It doesn't allow for the gray areas that make life real and complex.

For example:

- *"I always mess things up."* (Ignoring the times you've succeeded)
- *"I'll never get it right."* (Assuming that any mistake means failure)
- *"If I can't do it perfectly, there's no point in trying."* (The pressure of perfectionism)

This kind of thinking traps you in a cycle where you believe the worst about yourself or your situation. It makes challenges feel like dead ends, rather than stepping stones for growth. And it holds you back from seeing all the possibilities for change.

Blanket Statement: Covers Everything and Explains Nothing

A *blanket statement* is a broad, sweeping generalization. It's when we say something about ourselves or our lives that's way too all-encompassing. Instead of acknowledging the details and complexity, blanket statements treat everything like it's part of the same problem. For example:

- *"My life is a mess."* ➡ Is every part of your life really falling apart? Or just certain parts?
- *"Nothing ever works out for me."* ➡ Has literally *nothing* ever gone right for you, or is it just a tough time you're going through?
- *"I'm terrible at relationships."* ➡ Is that really true, or are there moments in your relationships that are positive?

The problem with blanket statements is that they trap you in a narrow, distorted view of yourself. They reduce complex moments of struggle into sweeping, limiting labels, turning temporary challenges into permanent aspects of your identity. This keeps you stuck, perpetuating negative thinking and self-doubt. That's why we need a "Moment of Truth" step in this transformational journey. It's the key to breaking free from those all-or-nothing beliefs and seeing yourself, and your potential, clearly.

Why Absolute Thinking and Blanket Statements Hold You Back

Both absolute thinking and blanket statements will have you believing that just because something's hard right now, it's always going to be that way. If you tell yourself, *"I always fail,"* why would you even try to succeed? If you say, *"I'm not good enough,"* how will you ever find the courage to push forward?

But here's the powerful truth: **You can change the story.** Once you realize you're doing this, you can shift those extreme blanket thoughts into more realistic, compassionate ones. Instead of *"I always fail,"* try

"I've faced setbacks, but I've also overcome challenges before." Instead of *"My life is a mess,"* try *"There are parts of my life I'm working on, but other parts are going well."*

Recognizing and challenging these limiting thoughts will free you to embrace a more balanced, open mindset, one that allows for growth, mistakes, and progress. It's not about being perfect; it's about moving forward, step by step. Breaking free from absolute thinking and blanket statements gives you the freedom to see your life with more clarity and hope. You start to realize that growth is possible, and even small steps can make a big difference.

This first step—***awareness***—can feel daunting, overwhelming even. I know because I've been there. If you had asked me in my early twenties to take inventory of my life, I might have said: *"I'm a mess. I always quit everything. I can't get it together."*

That was my story. My truth, or so I believed.

On the surface, the evidence felt overwhelming: I was dropping out of university classes. I was stuck in a painful cycle of bingeing and purging. I was buried under the shame of body dysmorphia. I couldn't seem to stay motivated, hold things together, or move forward.

I called it all failure. I told myself I was lazy. Undisciplined. A quitter. But none of that was the real story. The truth? I wasn't lazy; I was *terrified*—terrified of failing, terrified of being seen struggling, and terrified that if I couldn't be perfect, I'd be exposed as not good enough.

Every time I stepped outside my comfort zone and risked failing, I collapsed, not because I didn't care, but because my nervous system was in survival mode. So I turned to the only thing that felt safe: my coping cycle. I'd binge. I'd purge. I'd push my body to exhaustion. Until I was too drained to try... which "confirmed" the story that I wasn't capable. But that wasn't the truth. That was a **blanket statement** my mind clung to because the pain beneath it felt unbearable.

- *"I'm a quitter."*
- *"I'm a failure."*
- *"This is just who I am."*

What I couldn't see back then was that those stories weren't facts. They were protection. They simplified the complexity of my pain into something I could name, because naming it felt safer than feeling it.

But through deep, honest awareness, I began to peel back the layers. I realized I wasn't broken. I was scared. I didn't lack motivation. I lacked safety. I didn't quit everything. I just didn't have the emotional tools or support to stay when it got hard. And I wasn't weak. I was operating from a nervous system that equated failure with shame.

I had internalized the belief: *If I'm not perfect, I'm nothing.* And that belief didn't just shape my actions. It shaped my identity. Until I started telling the truth. That truth didn't just shift how I saw myself. **It gave me my life back.** Because when I stopped labeling myself and started listening to what was underneath, I could finally meet my pain with compassion instead of criticism. And that's when the healing began.

So if you're reading this, and you're struggling to see anything clearly... if you feel like everything's a blur and your story is too far gone, pause.

Take a breath.

You're not a mess. You're not hopeless. You're just standing too close to your pain to see the whole picture. That's why this step matters so much. Because once you start telling the truth, not the filtered version, not the one wrapped in shame or all-or-nothing thinking, you give yourself the chance to *see yourself clearly.* And that is always the beginning of *becoming.*

When Negativity Becomes the Room You Live In

If you've ever found yourself trapped in a cycle of negative thoughts...

"I'll never get this right." "People always disappoint me." "What's the point of even trying?"

... you're not alone.

Chronic negative thinking is one of the most overlooked forms of self-sabotage. And it's also one of the most convincing. Because it *feels* true. It feels familiar. It feels like protection, like if you expect the worst, you can't be hurt by it.

But here's what you might not realize: **Negative thinking doesn't just hurt you.** It can quietly hurt your relationships, too. When negativity becomes your baseline, it becomes your energy. And that energy is *felt* by everyone around you.

You may begin to notice people pulling away... conversations growing shorter... invitations disappearing... not because people don't care, but because being around unprocessed pain, unrelenting pessimism, or persistent complaints can feel **heavy** and **draining**. And if this has happened to you, if friendships have faded or people seem to keep their distance, it's time for one of the hardest and most healing questions you can ask yourself:

"Is it possible that my mindset is pushing people away?"

And it's not because you're bad. It's not because you're unworthy. But because the energy you bring into a space, whether it's hopeful or hopeless, curious or closed, *shapes the experience for everyone in it.*

We all have hard seasons. We all go through pain. But if negativity has become your identity, your default lens, your daily soundtrack, then people may not be rejecting *you.* They may be retreating from the heaviness that surrounds you. That awareness might sting at first. But it's also a gift. Because it gives you a starting point. It gives you a chance to shift.

This chapter isn't about shame. It's about truth. And the truth is: Negative thinking is not self-awareness. It's self-abandonment wrapped in the disguise of realism. It doesn't make you wise. It makes you weary. And it doesn't keep you safe. It keeps you *small...* and often, *alone.*

That's why this first step of the B.E.C.O.M.I.N.G. Formula, **awareness**, is so important. It asks you to gently disrupt the loop. To pause the spiral long enough to ask:

Is this really true? Or is this just what I've always thought?

It's not about "thinking positive." It's about thinking **honest. Specific. Curious. Alive.** Because awareness doesn't ask you to ignore what's hard. It asks you to *see clearly enough* that you can stop mistaking your pain for your identity.

It's time! Grab your pen and paper, beautiful soul. It's time to dive into your personal inventory!

You're ready to start your transformation. You're not just thinking about change; you're actively creating it. You are showing up, doing the work, and taking charge of your transformation. That, my friend, is powerful!

This inventory isn't a test. It's not a performance. And it's definitely not a place for perfection. It's a moment of *truth-telling*, not *self-judgment*.

You're not here to fix your whole life in one sitting. You're here to *see it*. Honestly. Lovingly. Without shame.

So as you begin...

- **Go gently.** If a question feels hard, pause. Breathe. Come back later.
- **Be specific.** Blanket statements like "Everything is a mess" will keep you stuck. Dig deeper. Find the *real* story.
- **Honor your progress.** You're not just naming what hurts, you're acknowledging what's working, too.
- **Expect emotion.** If grief, anger, or regret surfaces, that's okay. It means you're accessing something real. Stay with it.
- **You are not your answers.** What you write down today is not your identity. It's just information. Data. Awareness.

Welcome to Step One of B.E.C.O.M.I.N.G. Take out your companion workbook. If you haven't downloaded it yet, pause and do that now. This is the moment you move from reading about change to creating it. Let's get to work!

CHAPTER 10

B.E.C.O.M.I.N.G.

Embracing Accountability and Taking Ownership

"Freedom is the moment you stop waiting for someone else to change your life."

— Unknown

The Power of Accountability: Owning Your Story

This is the chapter where it all begins to change because this is where you stop outsourcing your power.

Breaking through limiting beliefs isn't just about awareness. It's not enough just to understand where they came from or who handed them to you. At some point, if you want to be free, you have to **take ownership of the part that's still holding on**. That's what accountability is. Not punishment. Not perfection. **Power.** It's the moment you decide to stop waiting for someone to apologize, to see you, to save you. It's the moment you realize:

"I can't change what happened, but I can absolutely change what I do next."

Real accountability is an act of radical self-respect. It says: *"I am no longer waiting to be chosen, rescued, or validated. I am choosing myself. I am choosing my healing."* You stop pointing to your childhood, your ex, your trauma, or your past and saying:

"This is why I'm stuck."

Those experiences may have shaped you. But they don't get to define you **unless you let them**. Because here's the raw, beautiful truth: **Your limiting beliefs may not be your fault, but they are your responsibility.** And when you embrace that? You stop living by the old scripts. You stop needing closure to move forward. You stop hoping someone else will hand you the life you crave. You become the one who *chooses* the life you crave.

This is the moment everything shifts. Because once you take ownership, you're no longer reacting to life, you're leading it. And yes it takes courage. Yes it asks you to stop running and numbing. Yes it asks you to look honestly at the life you've built, not by accident but **brick by brick**:

- Every "yes" you didn't mean.
- Every "no" you were too afraid to say.
- Every belief you absorbed before you knew you had a choice.

You may not have chosen every circumstance. But you have shaped your path, one decision at a time. And now? You get to shape what comes next. This is the moment you stop asking: *"Why is this happening to me?"* and start asking: *"What am I ready to create now?"*

So no, this step isn't always easy, but it's a pivotal one. Because accountability is not a burden. It's **liberation**. It's how you move from victimhood to vision, from reaction to authorship, from inherited beliefs… to intentional becoming.

Let this be the line in the sand…

"I may not have chosen the wound. But I choose the healing. And I choose it now."

If you're here to grow… If you're here to evolve… If you're ready to become the version of yourself you've only glimpsed in your quietest moments…

This is your turning point, not because someone told you it's time, but because something deep inside you knows you're ready. You don't need to be perfect. You don't need to have it all figured out. You just need to be willing. Present. And brave enough to say:

"I take responsibility for my life. All of it. Not because I have to…
But because I choose to. Because I'm worth it."

Embracing Accountability: The Antidote to Limiting Beliefs

Breaking free from limiting beliefs isn't just about recognizing them, it's about actively dismantling them. It's about creating an environment where your transformation isn't left to chance but instead becomes an inevitable outcome of your commitment. And one of the most powerful ways to ensure this? **Embracing accountability.**

Accountability is the bridge between *intention* and *action*, between *knowing* what needs to change and actually *changing* it. It's the unseen force that holds you to your highest potential, even when your old patterns try to pull you back into comfort and complacency.

Without accountability, limiting beliefs thrive. They whisper, "Not now. Maybe later." They convince you that staying the same is easier than stepping into the unknown. They tell you transformation is for *other* people, not for you. And if you're not careful, they'll keep you stuck in the same place for years, sometimes even a lifetime.

But here's the truth: Your future self is counting on you to show up today.

Excusitis: The Failure Disease That Keeps You Stuck

Dr. David Schwartz, in *The Magic of Thinking Big*, introduced the idea of *Excusitis, The Failure Disease.* It's the silent killer of potential, the subtle yet destructive habit of allowing excuses to take the driver's seat of your life. It sounds like:

"I just don't have the time right now."

"I've tried before, and it didn't work."

"I'm too old, too young, too inexperienced, too busy..."

"This is just who I am."

At first glance, these statements don't seem harmful. They don't sound like self-sabotage. In fact, they seem logical, even reasonable. But that's what makes *Excusitis* so dangerous. It disguises itself as truth when, in reality, it's just fear in a well-crafted costume. And at its core, *Excusitis* is simply **limiting beliefs in action.**

Every excuse you make is a belief about what you think is possible for you. Every justification for why you *can't* do something is a reflection of an unconscious story you've accepted as truth. The belief that you "don't have time" is really the *belief* that **your growth isn't a priority.** The belief that "this is just who I am" is really the *belief* that **you are incapable of change.** The belief that "I've tried before and failed" is really the *belief* that **failure is a stop sign rather than a stepping stone.** These beliefs are *not* facts. But the longer you let *Excusitis* run the show, the more they feel like unshakable truths.

And that's why accountability is the key to breaking free.

Accountability: The Key to Overriding Limiting Beliefs

In the B.E.C.O.M.I.N.G. Formula, this step is about **Embracing Accountability** because transformation doesn't happen in isolation. You cannot out-think your limiting beliefs. You must *out-act* them. And action requires accountability.

When you commit to accountability, you interrupt the cycle of limiting beliefs in real time. You replace "I'll do it later" with "I'm doing it now." You replace self-doubt with structured, measurable progress. You override fear with commitment. Why? Because accountability collapses the gap between intention and action.

Here's what that looks like in practice:

Excuse: "I don't have time to work on myself." *Embracing Accountability:* "I schedule non-negotiable time every day to work on my mindset, just like I would for an important meeting."

Excuse: "I've always been this way." *Embracing Accountability:* "I surround myself with people who challenge me to grow and reflect back my potential, not my past patterns."

Excuse: "I'm not confident enough." *Embracing Accountability:* "I commit to action, knowing that confidence isn't something you wait for, it's something you build through doing."

Breaking Free from the Blame Game

Let's be real: pointing fingers is easy. "I'd be successful *if* my boss wasn't so difficult." "I'd be happier *if* my partner just understood me better." "I'd go after my dreams *if* life wasn't so unfair." Sound familiar? We've all been there. Blame provides temporary relief, like junk food for the soul, satisfying in the moment but leaving you feeling worse in the long run.

The problem? When we blame external factors for our struggles, we give away our power. We hand over the pen that writes our life story and let circumstances, or worse, other people decide our fate. But here's the truth: you *can't* control everything that happens to you, but you *can* control how you respond. And that distinction is what separates those who remain stuck from those who rise above.

Viktor Frankl, a Holocaust survivor and the author of *Man's Search for Meaning*, put it best: "Between stimulus and response, there is a space. In that space is our power to choose our response. In our response lies our growth and our freedom."

That's the power of accountability; it shifts you from feeling powerless to realizing you have *options*. And with options comes freedom.

The Price of Avoiding Responsibility

What happens when you *don't* take responsibility for your life? You stay stuck. You keep repeating the same painful cycles, reliving the same arguments, and engaging in the same self-sabotage. You wake up with the same ache in your chest that whispers, *"There has to be more than this."*

Avoiding responsibility doesn't protect you; it *shrinks you.* It keeps you reacting instead of creating, drifting instead of deciding, existing instead of truly living. It's like handing over the keys to your life and then wondering why you never feel in control. You start to blame your past, your partner, your parents, your job, or your timing. And that is anything but the truth.

Slowly, without even realizing it, you begin to lose faith in yourself. You start believing the lie that maybe you're just stuck. That maybe change is for other people. But that's not the truth. That's the price of giving your power away. And that price? It's devastating.

You look up and realize a year has passed and nothing's different. Five years go by, and the pain you swore you'd heal is still running the show. A decade later, you're haunted by what could have been, if only you had said yes to yourself sooner.

Because here's what no one tells you: without accountability, nothing sticks. Without ownership, nothing changes. Without responsibility, your life becomes a slow leak of potential, draining you of time, confidence, connection, and peace.

So if you're feeling the weight of regret, the frustration of inertia, or the sting of watching your own potential pass you by, *let that pain mean something.* Let it wake you up. Not because you've failed, but because you're done pretending this is all there is.

You are not too far gone. It is not too late.

So take the wheel. Take the pen. Take your life back. Because the cost of waiting is always greater than the courage it takes to begin.

Mindfulness: Your Secret Weapon for Accountability

So, how do you *actually* shift into accountability?

Enter mindfulness, the art of paying attention without judgment. When you're mindful, you become aware of your choices in real time. You notice when you're making excuses. You catch yourself playing the victim. And instead of spiraling into self-pity, you pause and ask, *"How am I contributing to this situation?"*

Mindfulness shines a light on the patterns holding you back. It helps you see that your habits, thoughts, and reactions are *yours*, which means they can be changed. Instead of thinking, *"Why is this happening to me?"* you start asking, *"What can I do about this?"* And that's the turning point. That's when you reclaim control.

> "We cannot be blamed for the way our brains were wired in childhood. But as adults, we have the responsibility—and the capacity—to rewire them."
>
> – Gabor Mate

The same applies to every aspect of your life. You may not have caused every struggle you face, but you *are* responsible for how you move forward. Here's the bottom line: No one is coming to save you. That might sound harsh, but it's also liberating. Because if no one else is responsible for your happiness, success, or fulfillment, it means you are. And that's the best news possible. It means your future isn't dictated by your past. It means you're not stuck. It means you get to *choose.*

So, the next time you look in the mirror, don't just see your reflection. See your potential. See the person who has the power to rewrite their story. Because the moment you take full ownership of your life, the moment you decide to stop waiting and start creating, that's the moment everything changes.

The Reckoning Before the Rise: My Moment of Truth

Let's get one thing straight: I was not born with an accountability gene. If anything, I spent years dodging responsibility for my emotions, my choices, and the way my life was unfolding. I was pretty much a chronic blamer. I blamed. I resented. I justified my excuses. And for a long time, I didn't even realize I was doing it.

If I could go back and give my younger self one piece of advice, it would be this:

Own your life. Own your choices. Own your power. (... and invest in Microsoft.) I don't share my personal stories to entertain you, though if they make you smile, that's a bonus. I share them so you can see yourself in them. So you know you're not alone. I share them because I want to hand you the shortcuts I never had. If my struggles, my missteps, and the lessons I've learned the hard way can help you break free faster, with less pain and fewer detours, then every challenge I've faced has meaning. Every one of them has been worth it.

The fact is, healing doesn't have to be a slow, agonizing process. You don't have to stay stuck, lost, or searching for answers in the dark for decades. I've been there, and I want to light the path so you can walk it with more clarity, more confidence, and far less suffering.

You are *not* meant to stay tangled in old wounds. You are meant to rise, to reclaim your power, and to step boldly into the life you were always meant to live. If my stories can help you do that, then grab my hand because we're walking this road together.

The Hard Pill to Swallow

Accountability isn't just about responsibility, it's about freedom. And that freedom? It starts the moment you decide to stop blaming, stop making excuses, and start taking ownership of your life.

Let me take you back to the moment when I finally woke up to this truth.

In my early thirties, I was part of a remarkable group of women, a circle of soul sisters who met monthly for deep, soul-stirring conversations about growth, success, and manifestation. We called ourselves the Manifestation Group, though, in reality, it was just as much about personal breakthroughs, belly laughs, and lifting each other up as it was about books and vision boards. The wine flowed, the snacks were top-tier, and the wisdom? Life-changing.

These women? They were thriving. They were experiencing relationship and financial stability, two things I believed were lacking in my life. I felt like an outsider looking in.

At the time, I wasn't conscious of the toxic narrative playing on repeat in my mind, the shame stories about relationships, money, and success that had quietly dictated my life for years. I just knew one thing: Being around these women made me uncomfortable. But instead of pausing to ask myself *why?*... I did what so many of us do. I blamed and resented. I told myself that *they* were the problem. That *they* had something I didn't. And instead of seeing their success as evidence of what was possible for me, I let it deepen my insecurities and feed my resentment. So I did what fear and shame often drive us to do. I ran. I made excuses. I said I was *too busy.* I stepped back. And they wished me well and reminded me I was always welcome.

Then came the breaking point, the downward spiral. The next monthly meeting took place at a cottage by the lake, an evening filled with bonfires, laughter, and connection. Though I had chosen to step away from the group, I was still on the email list, and I watched as messages of gratitude poured in. Thank-yous to the hostess, reflections on the magic of the night, and echoes of a gathering I wasn't part of.

And that's when it happened. One tiny, insidious thought crept into my mind:

"They didn't invite me."

That thought latched onto an old wound, and within moments, it snowballed.

- *I'm not wanted.*
- *I don't belong.*
- *I'm not enough.*

Within 24 hours, I had convinced myself that I had been purposely excluded. That these women, the very ones who had embraced me, had abandoned me. I felt crushed. And when we're in pain, we often react instead of reflect. So I did what any hurt version of me would do. I sent an emotionally charged email to the group, expressing my deep sadness and feeling of exclusion. And here's the thing… I believed every single word I wrote.

Not long after hitting send, my phone rang. It was our group leader, a wise, grounded psychotherapist who had seen right through me. She wasn't angry. She wasn't defensive. She just asked: *"Can we meet?"*

By the time I sat across from her, I had spent a full day drowning in my own emotional storm. She looked me in the eye and gently asked: *"Did I do something to make you feel unwelcome or not valued?"* I opened my mouth, ready to confirm my worst fears… but I couldn't. Because the truth was, *she hadn't done a thing.* None of them had. Then, in the kindest yet firmest voice, she said something that changed my life: *"I love you. But you need to own your shit."*

There it was. My moment of truth.

The Turning Point

I sat there, stunned. She didn't coddle me. She didn't let me off the hook. Instead, she lovingly held up a mirror, one that forced me to see how much I had been hiding behind blame and how much I had been giving my power away by making others responsible for my pain. And in that moment, something clicked. I realized how deeply my limiting beliefs had dictated my life. I saw, with painful clarity, how much I had made *other people* responsible for my happiness. I had spent years waiting for circumstances to change, for people to behave differently, for external validation to tell me I was worthy.

But the truth? It was never about them. It was always about me. **And that was the best and hardest truth I had ever faced.**

I did the only thing I could do. I owned it. I took my power back. And let me tell you, that's when everything changed.

The Apology Tour

I called each of those women, one by one, and apologized. I told them the truth: that I had been projecting my own pain onto them. That I had let my unhealed wounds distort reality. And you know what happened? They welcomed me back with open arms. Because true connection? True sisterhood? It thrives on honesty.

I became deeply aware of every person and situation where I had shifted blame instead of taking responsibility. And with that realization, I made a decision. I was done giving away my power. It was time to own my part in every "blame" story I had rewritten. So, I embarked on what I now call my "apology tour," not just to make amends but to liberate myself in the process. Because taking ownership? It's *liberating.* It's *empowering.* It's the first step to taking your power back.

Here's what I know now: Accountability is not about guilt. It's the ultimate power move! It's about recognizing your beliefs and owning your thoughts, actions, and emotions as your responsibility and no one else's—not your past, not your circumstances, not anyone else.

When you invest in personal accountability, you stop being a victim and start being the author of your own life. That was the day I stopped waiting for permission to be happy.

And now? It's your turn. This is where you get the workbook out, my friend. Let's get to work!

CHAPTER 11

B.E.C.O.M.I.N.G.

Challenge the Conditioning, From Pattern to Possibility

> "Once is happenstance. Twice is coincidence. Three times is a pattern."
>
> —Ian Fleming

If you've ever asked yourself, *"Why does this keep happening?"*, you're in the right place.

Before we dive into breaking the beliefs that have held you back, we need to talk about the patterns that built them because limiting beliefs don't just appear out of nowhere. They're the result of repeated experiences, internalized messages, and survival strategies that, over time, became your default settings.

This chapter isn't about theory; it's about truth.

And here's one that might sting: if you don't identify the patterns running your life, they will continue to shape your choices, reactions, and results, without your permission. You might be thinking, *"I already know this stuff."* And maybe you do. But knowing something intellectually and *seeing it clearly enough to change it* are two very different things.

So I challenge you: Don't read this with autopilot eyes. Read it like your future depends on it. Because in many ways, it does. This is the chapter where things shift from passive awareness to powerful insight. Come to these words with fresh eyes, with a heart that's willing to get honest, and with the courage to dig deeper than you have before, not because you're broken or in need of fixing but because there is more of you waiting to be revealed. More freedom. More clarity. More truth.

Because the moment you clearly *see* the patterns that have been running your life quietly, automatically, beneath the surface, you take the first bold step in reclaiming the power to change them.

Patterns: The Blueprint Beneath It All

A pattern is anything you repeat, consciously or unconsciously, that creates results in your life. It's not just the habits you've formed or the actions you take. It's how you think, how you react, and how you interpret what happens around you. And over time, these internal repetitions begin to shape how you see yourself and what you believe is possible. They quietly build your identity, one thought, one emotional response, one internal dialogue at a time.

Some patterns lift you. They give you the courage to take action, the confidence to speak up, the resilience to keep going when things get hard. These are the mental and emotional frameworks that push you forward. A pattern of self-worth allows you to ask for what you deserve. A pattern of self-trust helps you take bold risks. A pattern of hope gives you the energy to keep showing up, even when you're not sure how things will turn out.

But not all patterns serve you. Some keep you stuck, trapped in hesitation, self-doubt, and fear. Maybe you've developed a pattern of playing small so others won't feel uncomfortable or a pattern of overthinking every decision because you're terrified of making the wrong one. Maybe you've convinced yourself you're not ready, not qualified, or not worthy. These aren't flaws in your character. They're mental loops and programmed responses based on past experiences. They're not who you are. They're just who you've been *taught* to be. And if they were learned, they can be unlearned.

These patterns are not random. They are the hidden blueprints of your inner world, the thought loops, emotional reflexes, and deeply rooted beliefs that were etched into your mind without your conscious permission. I'm not asking you to simply *understand* this. I'm asking you to *feel* the full weight of it. Because this isn't just about catching a negative thought once in a while. This is about waking up to the fact that the story you've been telling yourself over and over is either clearing the path toward your highest self or reinforcing the walls that keep you playing small.

Patterns are the invisible architecture of your life, the hesitation before you raise your hand, the tension in your chest before you speak your truth, and the inner critic that drowns out every compliment. These are the scripts running in the background. They shape the opportunities you pursue or reject. They influence how deeply you allow yourself to be loved. They determine how you treat yourself when no one's watching. If you've ever thought, *"Why do I keep ending up here?"*, this is why.

Here's what you need to know: Your thoughts aren't just random flickers of awareness. They're creative forces. They are the architects of your experience. They write the story you live. If you're not aware of them, if you're not consciously choosing them, you'll live the same story on repeat. Different faces. Different names. Different settings. But the same script.

And then you might start to believe, *"This is just who I am."* But what if it's not?

What if what you've accepted as your personality is actually just a pattern, one that formed out of survival, protection, or early conditioning? What if the version of reality you've been living in isn't *truth* but simply a script you didn't write? That's why we need to take a closer look at the stories you tell yourself because those stories aren't just shaping your thoughts... they're shaping your life.

These stories, the ones on repeat in your mind, become mental grooves that your brain follows automatically. They're formed through repetition, emotion, and experience. And the more often you think a certain way… *I'm not ready… I always mess this up… People can't be trusted…* the more your brain strengthens that pathway. Eventually, it becomes your default narrative. It starts to feel normal, familiar, and even true.

But here's the truth: just because a story feels familiar doesn't mean it's accurate. And it doesn't mean it's serving you.

What's powerful is this: your brain isn't fixed. It's built to change. Thanks to **neuroplasticity**, you now know that your brain rewires itself based on what you practice and repeat. That means every time you interrupt an old story and choose a new thought, you're not just shifting your mindset, you're physically changing your brain. This is the beginning of real transformation.

You don't have to battle every limiting belief. You just have to become aware of the story you're telling and decide if it's one that is serving you. Awareness disrupts the old pattern. Repetition creates a new one. And thought by thought, story by story, you begin showing up as someone who chooses how the next chapter unfolds. That's how we break the cycle. That's how we reclaim our power. You are not the story you've been telling yourself on autopilot. You're the author. You always have been. And the moment you realize that, truly realize it, you'll never look at yourself, or your future, the same way again.

Read this chapter not as information, but as revelation. Let it be a mirror that reflects what's really been holding you back, not because you're broken but because you've been running outdated programming. The moment you recognize that your patterns are not fixed but *flexible*, that they are not who you *are* but who you've *learned* to be, everything changes. This is the moment where awareness becomes your superpower.

Your thoughts are not facts. Do not believe everything you think.

Your thoughts are well-rehearsed mental habits, ones that have been playing in your mind for so long that you've stopped questioning them.

You don't have to stay in the loop. You don't have to repeat the same old story. You get to interrupt the pattern, challenge the belief, and write something new. You get to reclaim the pen. And from here forward, you get to become the author of a future that isn't built on fear or limitation but on power, purpose, and conscious choice.

Pattern vs. Cycle: What's the Difference?

Alright, let's break this down because patterns and cycles are not the same thing. They might seem interchangeable, but knowing the difference is key to getting unstuck.

Think of it this way: patterns influence your thinking, while cycles keep you trapped in repetition. One is the blueprint, and the other is the endless loop. Let me explain...

Patterns: Your Brain's Auto-Pilot Mode

A pattern is a habit, something you repeatedly think, feel, or do without even realizing it. It's like your brain's go-to setting, the mental shortcut it defaults to whenever a certain situation pops up. *Example of a Thought Pattern:* Every time you make a mistake, you immediately think, *"I always mess things up."* Over time, this repeated thought turns into a belief that you're just not capable. *Example of a Behavior Pattern:* Whenever you feel overwhelmed, you procrastinate instead of taking action. This reaction becomes your automatic response to stress, keeping you stuck in avoidance. Patterns don't necessarily create repetition in your actual life... yet. But they shape how you see the world, react to situations, and make decisions.

Cycles: The Never-Ending Replay Button

A cycle happens when a pattern starts running the show so much that it creates the same results over and over again. It's when you keep finding yourself in the same frustrating situations, thinking, *"Why does this keep happening to me?" Example of a Negative Cycle:* You believe *"I'm not good enough."* (**thought pattern**) Because of this belief, you avoid speaking up or going after opportunities. (**behavior pattern**) As a result, you don't get ahead, which reinforces the belief that you're not good enough. (**boom, cycle locked in!**)

See the difference? A pattern is just a repeated thought or behavior. But when that pattern starts playing out in your real life, trapping you in the same loop, it's officially a cycle. Still not sure you get it? Let's try another example that may just hit closer to home: Relationship patterns and cycles.

Patterns vs. Cycles in Toxic Relationships

Let's talk about toxic relationships because if you've ever found yourself stuck in one (or several), chances are there's a pattern at play. And if it keeps happening? You're caught in a cycle.

A pattern in relationships is the way you think, feel, or behave when it comes to love, connection, and self-worth. It's the inner programming that dictates what you tolerate, how you show up, and what you expect from others. *Example of a Relationship Pattern:* You grew up feeling like you had to "earn" love, so you believe that love = proving your worth. Because of this, you tend to over-give, ignore red flags, or settle for less than you deserve.

When someone is emotionally unavailable or treats you poorly, you rationalize it, thinking, *"I just need to love them harder, and they'll change."* At this stage, it's still just a pattern, a subconscious way of thinking and behaving that influences your relationships.

A cycle is when this pattern keeps creating the same type of relationship over and over again. You might think, *"Why do I always attract the wrong people?"* or *"Why does this keep happening to me?"* The truth is, it's not just about attraction. It's about unconscious repetition.

How it all plays out in your life...

You get involved with someone who is emotionally unavailable, inconsistent, or toxic, and you pour yourself into fixing or proving your worth in the relationship. The other person doesn't change, and you end up feeling unappreciated, drained, or hurt. The relationship falls apart, and you tell yourself, *"I'll never end up in this kind of situation again."*

Time passes, but you haven't addressed the pattern, so you unknowingly fall for the same type of person. Rinse and repeat. If this sounds familiar, it's not bad luck. It's a cycle. And here's the real kicker: until you notice the pattern driving the cycle, you'll keep repeating it with different people in different ways. The faces may change, but the outcome stays the same.

Thought Patterns vs. Behavioral Patterns: What's the Difference?

If you're serious about breaking free from limiting beliefs, you need to understand the difference between *thought patterns* and *behavioral patterns*. Because here's the thing: thoughts drive behavior. And if you only focus on changing what you *do* without changing how you *think*, you'll find yourself back in the same cycle, again and again.

Thought patterns are the inner stories you repeat to yourself often unconsciously. They sound like:

- *"I'm not good enough."*
- *"I always mess things up."*
- *"Success isn't meant for people like me."*

These aren't facts. They're mental habits and internal scripts you've picked up along the way, shaped by past experiences, old wounds, or voices from your childhood. Left unchallenged, these thoughts become the lens through which you interpret your entire life. They color your confidence, dim your dreams, and quietly set limits on what you believe is possible.

Behavioral patterns are the actions you take or don't take based on those inner stories. They're the choices you make on autopilot, often without realizing they're rooted in belief systems that no longer serve you. For example, if your inner narrative says, *"I'm not good enough,"* your behavior follows suit. You hold back. You play small. You talk yourself out of applying for the job, speaking your truth, or setting the boundary, not because you can't but because somewhere deep down, you've already decided it's not meant for you.

Behavior follows belief. Always.

This is the cycle that traps so many people and keeps them stuck for years. It starts with a thought, something small and seemingly harmless. You make a mistake, maybe a typo in an email, stumble in a conversation, or forget a deadline. Instead of brushing it off, an old whisper surfaces: *"I always mess things up."* And in that moment, your brain doesn't stop to ask if it's true. It doesn't sift through evidence with logic or perspective. It just *believes* you. And then it goes looking for proof. It becomes the judge, jury, and prosecutor, digging through your mental archives for every misstep you've ever made, every failure, every flaw, every moment of doubt. It stacks the deck against you until one thought becomes a belief:

"This isn't just something I did. This is who I am."

And that belief? It becomes the compass for your actions. You pull back. You doubt yourself. You silence your voice in meetings, downplay your ideas, and settle for less than you deserve. You stop chasing what excites you and start shrinking to fit a mold that was never meant for you. You miss opportunities, not because you aren't ready and not because you're not worthy. But because your *actions* begin to mirror your *beliefs*, and your life starts to reflect those choices. And when things don't go your way, your brain points to the outcome and says, *"See? I told you so."* The cycle continues. The pattern repeats. The belief solidifies. And soon, you don't just think it's true, you *know* it's true, even though it never really was.

This is how people stay stuck, not because they're lazy, not because they lack discipline or ambition, but because they don't recognize the loop. They're pressing play on the same mental script, hoping for a new ending, but never changing the story.

Until now. Because now, you're becoming aware. Now, you're learning how to press *stop*. And awareness? That's everything. Because once you *see* the pattern, you gain the power to interrupt it, to challenge the thought, rewrite the belief, and choose a different action.

This is the beginning of freedom. You're not just changing your behavior, but you're transforming the belief that drives it. And that is how you change your life, from the inside out.

What Shapes the Stories You Tell Yourself?

Every thought has a beginning. It's not random. It's triggered by something. Sometimes it's subtle, a passing observation that barely registers. But other times, a thought hits deeper. It lingers. It loops. And before you know it, it's become a story you tell yourself so often, it starts to feel like truth.

If you don't stop to question where these thoughts come from, you can end up spending years, maybe even a lifetime living under the weight of beliefs that were never really yours to begin with. So what inspires these internal stories? And how do we reclaim control over the ones that no longer serve us?

1. Your Past: The Lens You're Still Looking Through

Your brain stores every experience, every success, every failure, and every moment of love, pain, embarrassment, or joy. Think of it as your invisible "life backpack," filled with everything you've ever lived through. And like it or not, your brain uses what's in that pack as a filter for every new situation.

That's how thought patterns begin. You're not always seeing life as it is, you're seeing it through the lens of past wounds, past disappointments, and past programming.

If your backpack is packed with failure or rejection, your brain will whisper, *"Don't try. It won't work out."* If it's filled with memories of not being enough, your mind will default to stories like, *"See? You never measure up."* And just like that, you hesitate. You stay quiet. You settle, not because you're not capable but because your patterns convinced you that you aren't. The most dangerous part? It all happens without you realizing it.

You don't just remember the past. You live through it, see through it, and judge yourself through it, unless you pause and ask, *"Is this belief helping me, or is it holding me back?"* If it's the latter, it's time to unpack the stories that are weighing you down and make room for something new.

2. Your Environment: The Voices You've Absorbed

Not every thought in your head belongs to you. Let that sink in.

Many of the beliefs you carry about success, love, worth, and identity weren't consciously chosen. They were inherited, absorbed, and handed down by others when you were too young to question them. Maybe it was a parent telling you to "be realistic," a teacher who made you feel small, or a society that taught you to shrink, conform, or stay silent. And without realizing it, you accepted those words as truth. You didn't ask for them. You didn't agree to them. But you carried them anyway.

The good news? You don't have to keep carrying what isn't yours. You are not obligated to believe every thought that crosses your mind. You get to decide what stays and what goes. You get to rewrite the script.

3. Your Mood: The Filter That Distorts Your View

Let's not forget the power of emotion. Sometimes your thoughts aren't reflecting your truth; they're just reflecting your *mood.*

When you're energized, hopeful, and feeling good, your thoughts expand: "*I've got this. I can figure it out. Anything is possible.*" But when you're tired, stressed, or discouraged, those same thoughts can shrink to "*Why bother? I'm not good enough. Nothing's working.*" Your emotional state colors everything.

So the next time you catch yourself spiraling into doubt, pause. Take a breath. Ask yourself, *"Is this my truth? Or is this just my mood talking?"* Because moods are temporary. But the stories you repeat become beliefs. And beliefs shape your reality unless you challenge them.

Bottom line... Your thoughts are shaped by your past, your environment, and your emotional state. But they are not set in stone. You get to question them. You get to choose differently. You get to tell a new story, one that actually reflects your strength, your potential, and your truth.

And when you do? Everything changes.

Heuristics: The Mental Shortcuts Behind the Patterns

By now, you know that patterns are everywhere—in your thoughts, your habits, your decisions. But what you may not know is that your brain has been reinforcing these patterns *automatically,* often without your awareness.

Enter: **heuristics.**

If we've worked together before, you've probably heard me nerd out over this term at least a thousand times. Why? Because heuristics are *everywhere.* These mental shortcuts shape the way you think, react, and interpret the world, often without you even realizing it. And yes... we're going *there* again. Because truly understanding heuristics is a game-changer when it comes to breaking free from limiting beliefs.

Think of heuristics like your brain's version of autopilot. It scans a situation, compares it to the past, and then responds quickly. Efficient? Yes. Accurate? Not always. At their best, heuristics are helpful. They're what allow you to drive a car, brush your teeth, avoid touching a hot stove, or recognize danger without having to stop and analyze every detail. But when those same shortcuts are applied to your *thoughts and beliefs,* especially the painful ones, they can quietly turn into traps.

Here's how it usually plays out:

One failure ➡ *"I'm not good at this."*

One heartbreak ➡ *"I can't trust anyone."*

One criticism ➡ *"I'm not smart enough."*

One rejection ➡ *"I'm just not lovable."*

And just like that, your brain stamps a label on the moment, files it in your backpack under "Truth," and carries it forward, recycling it every time a similar situation arises. You don't stop to question it because your brain thinks it's saving you time, pain, or energy. But what is it really doing? **Reinforcing the very beliefs that keep you stuck.** It's a pattern-forming machine.

Here's the real kicker... ready for it? Once your brain decides a belief is true, it stops looking for anything that might prove it wrong. It's like, *"Case closed. Moving on."* No more investigating. No more second-guessing. Sound familiar? Yes! **Confirmation bias**. We talked about this earlier, and look at you, remembering it! Seriously, you're crushing this.

It's that sneaky brain filter that only lets in the evidence that supports what you already believe, while quietly ignoring anything that contradicts it. It's helpful when you're scanning for danger but not so helpful when you're trying to grow beyond a belief like *"I'll never be good enough."* Because your brain? It'll just keep playing the same old highlight reel of failures and setbacks while conveniently skipping over your wins.

And that's how these patterns get locked in, quietly, automatically, and totally out of sight. You believe you're bad at relationships? You'll notice every failed one and ignore the healthy connections. You believe success isn't for you? Every setback becomes proof while every win is chalked up to luck or fluke. You believe you're not smart enough? Your mind will filter out every competent moment and highlight every fumble.

Your brain doesn't mean to sabotage you. It's just trying to be *efficient*. But in doing so, it reinforces beliefs that no longer serve you. Here's your wake-up call:

Your heuristics are not facts.

Your mental shortcuts can be rewritten.

You are not doomed to keep thinking the way you always have.

The moment you start noticing the shortcuts is the moment you take your power back. And from there, you get to choose which paths to stop walking and which new ones to create. You set goals, make promises to yourself, and swear *this time* will be different... but before you know it, you're right back where you started, repeating the same habits, facing the same frustrations, and questioning whether real change is even possible.

That's why paying attention to patterns and challenging the conditioning is a non-negotiable step in the BECOMING Formula. Because here's the deal: *you can't change what you're not aware of.* If you're trying to rewrite limiting beliefs without first understanding the thought and behavior patterns fueling them, it's like trying to fix a leak without knowing where the water's coming from.

Picture it like this: you're stumbling around in a pitch-black room, bumping into furniture and getting frustrated because you don't know what's in your way. You might even start to believe you're trapped. But then someone flips the light on. Suddenly everything is clear. You see the layout, you see the obstacles, and now you know exactly how to move forward.

That's what noticing patterns does. **It turns on the lights.**

Without that awareness, breaking free becomes nearly impossible. The same invisible walls will keep rising up in different forms—relationships, career, health—until you finally *see* them for what they are. Because every limiting belief is part of a larger loop, a script you've been running for years, sometimes decades. Until you recognize the pattern, it will keep writing your story for you.

But the second you spot it? **You reclaim your pen.** You move from autopilot to intention. You shift from reaction to conscious choice. You start creating instead of just coping. Think of awareness as the light switch in that dark room. The pattern, the belief, the cycle, it's been there all along, silently steering your choices. But once the light's on? You can't unsee it. You can finally do something about it. That's why awareness is the *entry point* to transformation.

So, this chapter isn't just about learning, it's about *seeing.* It's about becoming radically aware of the thoughts and behaviors that have quietly shaped your reality, so you can finally break the cycle and choose something better. Because once you understand the power of your patterns, you'll never see yourself, or your potential, the same way again.

The real issue isn't the belief itself. It's the fact that until now, it's been running the show behind the scenes. But now you see it. Now, you get to choose.

- You don't have to believe every thought that crosses your mind.
- You don't have to follow every old script your past handed you.
- You don't have to stay on autopilot.

From this moment forward, you get to lead, with intention, with clarity, with power. Creating a new reality starts with shifting your inner one. When you begin to notice the thought patterns driving your behaviors, you take back the reins. You stop living by default and start designing a life that actually serves you.

Remember, *you are not your thoughts.* You are the thinker. The author. The creator of your story. And the moment you choose to rewrite that story? You step into a world of limitless possibility. So take a breath. Trust your ability to change. And start noticing the patterns that have been quietly shaping your life. This is the moment you begin to break free. And just in case you need the reminder:

You are not your past.

You are not your patterns.

You are not stuck.

You are powerful.

You are capable of change.

And you are already rewriting your story. Let's do this! Grab your inner highlighter. It's time to rewrite your story! It's workbook time!

CHAPTER 12

B.E.C.O.M.I.N.G.

Own the New Vision

"It's not what the vision is, it's what the vision does."

—Peter Senge

As I sit down to write this chapter, my heart feels tender and open. My mom is entering a sacred stretch of her journey. We've recently learned that the cancer has returned, this time more aggressive and unrelenting. The path ahead looks different now. Though she remains full of spirit, surrounded by the unwavering love of those who cherish her, I can feel the quiet weariness in her body.

And so, the sacred work before us is clear: to hold these remaining days and months in a space of deep peace, unconditional love, and as much laughter as we can gather and to create a sanctuary of presence, where moments are not rushed, where small things matter, where love is not just felt, but *lived.*

I won't pretend this is easy. There are moments when the ache in my chest catches me off guard. Time feels slippery, fleeting, sacred. But this time, I'm meeting it differently. I'm not drowning in fear or unraveling in grief. I am *here*. Fully. And that presence, grounded, grateful, and awake, is the most profound gift I can offer her... and myself.

Because I've done the inner work, because I've allowed myself to feel, to heal, and to grow, I now meet this moment not with fear or emotional depletion but with a heart full of love and profound gratitude. I can show up for her in a way I never could before, not as a fixer, not as someone frantically trying to control the uncontrollable, but as a daughter simply loving her mother through every precious, ordinary moment.

If you've not yet grasped the extraordinary power of healing, of breaking free from the beliefs that keep you trapped in cycles of fear, scarcity, or self-doubt, let this be your invitation. You *deserve* to know this peace. You deserve to live from overflow, not survival. You deserve to love fully, to give deeply, and to receive life in all its beauty.

This work matters, not because it shields us from pain but because it expands our capacity to meet life with grace, courage, and clarity when it matters most. Wherever you are on this path, I want you to know: You are worthy of joy. You are worthy of healing. You are worthy of *this* level of love, for yourself and for those you hold dear.

So take a breath. Feel your feet on the ground. And let's continue this journey together, hand in hand, heart to heart. No better time than now.

Let's get back to work, with purpose, and with love.

Own the New Vision—The O in B.E.C.O.M.I.N.G.

Alright, now that you've challenged some of the limiting beliefs that kept you playing small, it's time to swing the door wide open to something so much bigger: your vision. This is where we start dreaming out loud, unapologetically. This is where you give yourself permission to envision a life that lights you up, one that aligns with your soul's deepest desires. Because now that you know you're capable of real, lasting change, the question becomes: *What do you want that change to look like?*

Let me be clear, defining your vision is not about creating some Pinterest-perfect fantasy life. This isn't about aesthetics or chasing someone else's dream. This is about clarifying what *you* truly want, not what you've been told to want. It's about reconnecting with your inner compass and charting a course that's deeply personal, purposeful, and powerful. This is your soul getting a voice.

Vision is the art of seeing what's possible, not in spite of your current circumstances but because you've reached the point where you're ready to rise above them. And here's what this healing journey has taught me, what I've come to believe with every fiber of my being: ***You were given this life because you are not only strong enough to live it, but brave and visionary enough to transform it.*** These words have never felt more true to me than they do right now, and my deepest wish is that they feel just as true for you.

Clarifying Your Vision: Dare to Dream Big (Yes, Really!)

Here's the thing: if your vision doesn't make your heart pound, your breath catch, or your voice shake a little when you speak it out loud, *it's not big enough.* A soul-aligned vision isn't supposed to feel safe. It's meant to stretch you, stir something inside you, and pull you toward the edge of who you thought you were.

The right vision will electrify your spirit and rattle your comfort zone. It'll light a fire in your belly, give you goosebumps, and make your palms sweat, not because you're not ready but because *you finally are.* It should feel thrilling, a little terrifying, and completely undeniable.

This is the dream that wakes you up, that won't let you settle. This is the dream that demands you rise. And it's waiting for you to say yes.

You know, like writing a self-help book that has the power to reach millions… It's bold. It's vulnerable. It's putting your heart and soul on full display, trusting that your story, your voice, your *truth* can spark transformation in someone else's life. Trust me, my palms get a little sweaty even as I write these words. But I know, deep in my bones, *this* is the vision. And when the vision is that clear, you don't wait for confidence. You lead with courage.

Now is the time to dream big and get as specific as you want. If you could design your life without limitations—no fear, no doubt, no "*What if I fail?*"...

- Where would you live?
- Who would be beside you?
- What would your days be filled with?
- How would you *feel* as you moved through your life?

Let your imagination go wild. Paint it in color, in texture, in the language of joy, and with total freedom. Picture it until you can feel it in your bones. Let it come alive so clearly that you can taste it. This is your blueprint, your internal GPS. Without it, you're just spinning in circles hoping to land somewhere good. Let's be intentional instead.

Don't worry about the *how* yet. That's dream-killing territory when you're just starting. Right now we're focused on the *what* and the *why*. Ask yourself:

- What does success mean to me?
- What lights me up?
- What kind of legacy do I want to leave?
- What do I want to experience in this lifetime?

And remember, there are no wrong answers. Your vision is yours alone. Own it. Protect it. Nurture it like a sacred seed planted in fertile soil. The world needs what only you can dream into being.

Awareness: The Secret Ingredient

Visions evolve. So do you. And that's a beautiful thing.

Awareness is the secret sauce that keeps your vision alive and aligned. It's the daily practice of checking in with yourself. *Does this still feel true for me? Is this vision still aligned with who I am becoming?*

Because here's the thing: you are a living, breathing work of art in progress. As you grow, heal, learn, and expand, what once lit you up might begin to dim. And that's not failure, that's evolution. Awareness allows you to realign, to shift gracefully rather than crumble in confusion. It gives you the power to adapt your vision to match the rising version of yourself.

Creating a vision isn't about setting your future in stone. It's about building a living, breathing relationship with your highest self. When you stay aware, open to change, and tuned in to your inner wisdom, you allow your vision to grow as you grow. And that is when life starts to feel truly aligned and wildly fulfilling. So stay awake. Stay curious. Keep dreaming. Keep evolving.

You deserve a life that sets your soul on fire. And you have everything within you to create it.

What If I Don't Know My Purpose?

First, take a breath. If you're asking this question, it means you're already on the path. It means something inside you is waking up and longing for more, and that is sacred.

Let me tell you something I've learned. Purpose isn't always a lightning bolt. It doesn't always show up with a grand announcement or a neon sign pointing the way. Sometimes, purpose whispers. It reveals itself slowly, in the spaces where your curiosity meets your courage. It lives in the things that light you up, the injustices that break your heart, and the moments when you feel most like *you*. So if you're unsure what your purpose is, begin here:

- **Follow what pulls at your heart.** What do you love? What makes you lose track of time? Purpose often hides in your passion.
- **Look at your pain.** What have you overcome? What lessons have shaped you? So often, our deepest wounds become the birthplace of our greatest gifts.
- **Pay attention to where you feel most alive.** Not just comfortable, but *alive.* Purpose thrives where authenticity lives.
- **Get quiet.** In a noisy world, purpose speaks in stillness. Make space to listen, through journaling, meditation, nature, or prayer.
- **Take small aligned steps.** You don't find purpose

by figuring it all out. You find it by living, by showing up, trying, learning, and staying curious.

And here's something really important—*limiting beliefs love to disguise themselves as facts* when it comes to purpose. They'll whisper things like:

- "You're not special enough."
- "You missed your chance."
- "You're too late, too broken, too average."

But none of that is true. Those are just old, tired narratives trying to keep you small. Your purpose doesn't require perfection. It simply asks for presence, for willingness, for a heart that says, "*I'm ready to explore.*" You don't have to find your purpose like it's lost. You're already holding the threads. Your purpose is not out there waiting to be discovered; it's in *you*, waiting to be remembered.

Be gentle with yourself. Trust the unfolding. And keep asking the question, not with frustration but with reverence. I'm inviting you to treat your search for purpose as a sacred unfolding rather than a problem to be solved. This is a gentle reminder that curiosity, longing, and growth are worthy of respect and patience. I know… easier said than done. Trust me, I know.

The very asking is proof that your soul is ready for the answer. Get ready to receive.

Roll up your sleeves, it's workbook time!

CHAPTER 13

B.E.C.O.M.I.N.G.

Meet Your Becoming

> "What we call the future self is really the nervous system in a state of trust."
>
> — Inspired by Joe Dispenza's work on neuroplasticity and identity

Embodying Your Future Self

I'll admit this was the chapter I wrestled with the most, only because I've grown to deeply appreciate the importance of taking action, how vital it is for transformation and how it's the turning point between knowing and becoming. However, every time I sat down to write it, something felt off. I kept circling around the same question: *How do I inspire action without feeding the very beliefs this book is helping to dismantle?* I went back and forth on the title, unsure how to capture what this chapter truly needed to say. Was it about action? Was it about worth? Could it be both?

And then it hit me, the truth of it: **you can't sustain action without self-worth**. You can start, yes. You can launch into something with adrenaline, with fear, even with desperation. But if you don't believe, deep down, that you are worthy of the results you're working toward, you will sabotage. You will shrink. You will burn out. Because action without worth is survival. But action *rooted* in worth? That's power. That's embodiment. That's the moment your healing stops living in your head and starts living in your life.

That's when I knew this chapter wasn't about choosing between self-worth or stepping into action. It was about **honoring the sacred relationship between the two**. One feeds the other. One unlocks the other. And together? They change everything.

So here goes...

There comes a moment in every healing journey when insight is no longer enough. When knowing isn't cutting it. When you've cried the tears, underlined the quotes, journaled through the hard parts, and still, something in you whispers, not quietly but with urgency: *It's time.* Time to rise. Time to move. Time to stop imagining the life you want and start experiencing it.

But here's the truth that doesn't always make it into the self-help highlight reels: you cannot step into lasting action from a place of unworthiness. You can't build a liberated, thriving life on the shaky ground of shame and self-doubt. Because we will *always* sabotage what we don't believe we deserve.

That's why, before we move forward, we have to root deeply into one unshakable truth: **you are worthy of the vision you hold.** This is the sacred threshold, the space where self-worth transforms into self-honoring action. One can't thrive without the other. Because without that foundation, all your beautiful healing and all your insight and growth risks staying trapped in the realm of theory. Understood, but never fully lived.

Self-worth is not a fleeting feeling. It's not confidence, not pride, not even self-esteem. It's a quiet, unshakable *knowing.* It's the foundation beneath your boundaries, the heartbeat behind your decisions, and the steady drum that says, even when life is messy, "I am still worthy." It's not earned. It's remembered. And for many of us, remembering our worth is the most radical act of our lives.

For me, that remembering didn't happen all at once. It was gradual, like soft light pouring through the cracks of everything I had once believed. I had spent years measuring my value by how much I could give, how productive I was, how thin I stayed, and how selfless I could become. Worth, to me, was a moving target, a performance, an exhausting game I never seemed to win.

I didn't know then what I know now: that worth doesn't come from what you do. It comes from who you *are* when all the proving and performing stops. It was there all along, beneath the eating disorders, beneath the people-pleasing, beneath the fear of taking up space. But I couldn't access it until I was willing to stop abandoning myself.

That's the invitation here, to come home to yourself and to return not to some perfect version of you but to the part that's always known the truth: *you were never broken.* You've only ever been buried under the weight and debris of beliefs that were never yours to carry.

This is what we mean when we say reclaiming your worth. It's not about becoming more. It's about peeling back everything that told you you were less. And once that remembering begins to take root, once that tiny ember of worth is reignited, there is only one thing left to do—*act like it, embody it.*

Because here's what I've learned: self-worth doesn't stay alive in theory. It must be lived, expressed, and put into motion. You don't reinforce your worth by simply writing in your journal or walking in nature. You reinforce it by speaking your truth when it's uncomfortable, by resting when you used to push, and by choosing peace over performance. Every single choice becomes a statement: *I know who I am now.*

But let's be honest, this is where many people get stuck. They wait to act until they feel ready, until the fear goes away, or until they've earned their way into action. But here's the secret: action is not the *reward* for healing. It's part of the healing. You don't wait for clarity to move. You create clarity by moving. You don't wait to feel brave to speak your truth. You build bravery *by speaking it.*

There is no perfect time. There is only now.

The version of you who's waiting for the stars to align, who's holding back until they're more confident, more healed, or more "together," they mean well. They're just scared. They are just trying to keep you safe. But they're not the one who will lead you into your desired self. That role belongs to the version of you who remembers, the one who knows their worth even when their voice shakes, the one who acts *as if* they're already enough, because they are.

So what does that look like in real life? It looks like saying no without the long explanation to justify. It looks like sending the email, having the conversation, setting the boundary, or applying for the thing that both terrifies and excites you. It looks like choosing to rest even when your to-do list screams at you. It looks like making art, making noise, taking up space, and letting that be *enough.*

It doesn't have to be dramatic. You don't need to turn your life upside down today. You just need to take one step, one small, brave, aligned step that says: *I know who I am. And I'm not hiding anymore.* Because here's the truth I want you to tattoo on your soul: you don't have to feel 100% ready to act. You just have to believe you're worth the effort. That is the shift.

But know that this step isn't about total transformation, and it's definitely not about perfection. It's about *practice.* It's about trying on your becoming like a new pair of shoes, not to impress anyone but to see how they feel as you start to move differently. It's about gradually stretching the edges of your comfort zone, not catapulting yourself so far out that your nervous system slams the brakes.

I know this because I've tried the all-or-nothing route. I've sprinted out of the gate, expecting to become the next version of myself overnight... only to crash and burn under the weight of the pressure I created. Real embodiment doesn't happen like that. *It's not a leap; it's a layering.*

Think of this phase like learning to walk again but with more wisdom, more clarity, and more intention than ever before. You're not here to sprint to the finish line. You're here to build the strength to keep going, to show up consistently, and to let your nervous system *trust* the new steps you're taking.

So let this be your permission to simply experience without judgement, to stumble, and to try again. Because every step you take in the direction of your vision, no matter how small, is a victory! It's a breakthrough. That is the moment everything begins to change, not just in your mind but in your body, your energy, your relationships, and your choices.

This is the work that matters most, the quiet, unglamorous, powerful work of repetition, presence, and progress.

The Key to Lasting Transformation: Action as the Catalyst

You know by now that transformation doesn't happen in your head. Insight alone won't change your life. Journaling is powerful. Reflection is essential. But real, embodied change? That only happens when you act.

Taking action is the cornerstone of personal transformation. It's how those lightbulb moments become lived truths. Action turns insight into embodiment. But more than that, it builds momentum, momentum that begins to move you out of your stuck places and into possibility.

And yet, fear and resistance have a way of showing up the moment we're about to change. Resistance will whisper, "Now's not the time." Fear will say, "What if you fail?" They'll try to convince you that you're not ready. But fear isn't the enemy; it's a signpost. It means you're doing something that matters. It means you're pushing beyond the limits of your old identity. It means growth is already underway. Welcome the discomfort and choose to move through it. Reframe fear. Let it be your cue, not to stop but to lean in. Let it fuel you instead of freeze you.

The magic lies in movement. Transformation requires *doing*, no matter how small the step. When you act, you build trust with yourself. You begin to see that you are not powerless, you are powerful. And that belief? That belief changes everything.

Most inaction is rooted in limiting beliefs, not laziness, not lack of discipline, but old stories that say, "I can't," or "I'm not ready," or "Who am I to…?" These beliefs keep you paralyzed. Stuck. But here's the good news: awareness breaks that cycle. The moment you see the belief for what it is—a lie you were taught, not a truth you have to carry—you begin to reclaim your power.

And then you move, one brave decision, one small step, one act of self-respect. That's all it takes to shift the trajectory of your life.

The 1% Rule

For years, I believed change had to be big and dramatic. All-or-nothing. Go big or go home. I'd get fired up, commit to overhauling my life overnight—new habits, new mindset, new me—and within days, I'd crash under the weight of my own expectations. My nervous system, especially with ADHD in the mix, would short-circuit with too many changes too fast.

It wasn't until I began embracing the **1% Rule** that things started to shift, gently, in a way I could actually sustain. The 1% Rule is simple but profound: just improve by 1% each day. That's it. No overhauls. No perfectionism. Just a slow, steady accumulation of self-respect.

One more glass of water.

One kinder thought.

One healthy boundary.

One moment of slowing down when your brain wants to speed up.

For someone like me, living with ADHD, this was a revelation (that, my friends, is a whole other book). I needed progress that didn't feel overwhelming. I needed wins that didn't require flawless follow-through. This rule allowed me to *move*, even when my executive functioning was struggling, even when my motivation was in hiding.

The truth? Those tiny shifts, the ones I once dismissed, became the foundation of my healing. The 1% Rule met me where I was. And it helped me build a life rooted not in urgency but in deep, sustainable change.

The Ripple Effect of Action

For all of us, momentum is everything, and so is *gentle recovery* when momentum breaks. And trust me, it will.

I hear you asking, "What does that even mean?"

Such a beautiful question, and such an important concept, especially for those of us wired for intensity, all-or-nothing thinking, or navigating ADHD, trauma healing, or just… being human. "Gentle recovery when momentum breaks" means: You don't punish yourself when you pause. You don't spiral into shame when you slow down. You don't let one skipped step become a reason to stop entirely. Instead, you meet yourself with compassion. You *re-enter* your path softly instead of tearing yourself apart for stepping off it. It means:

- Picking up where you left off without the guilt trip.
- Recognizing that rest, overwhelm, distraction, or regression don't erase your progress.
- Reminding yourself that consistency isn't perfection, it's *returning* again and again.
- Treating your healing like a relationship, not a performance.

For example: Maybe you had a strong week of nourishing meals, movement, and journaling, and then one day you crash. You're exhausted. You check out. You forget. Old patterns creep in. The old you might say, *"See? You never follow through. You always mess it up."*

Gentle recovery says: *"It's okay. You're still healing. Come back. We'll continue moving from here, without shame."*

It's the difference between starting over and simply *starting again*.

Learning to practice gentle recovery when momentum breaks was nothing short of transformational in my own journey to healing. It changed everything. It showed me that I didn't need to be perfect to grow, that I didn't have to earn my way back into healing, and that slipping didn't mean starting over; it simply meant returning.

This shift was radical for me. As someone who had lived with a food addiction, perfectionism, ADHD, and a deep fear of failure, the idea that I could pause without punishing myself was revolutionary. That I could meet myself in the dip with kindness instead of criticism? That was a homecoming.

Gentle recovery taught me that consistency isn't about never falling; it's about trusting yourself to rise, again and again, with love. And that truth has been and continues to be one of the most healing gifts of my entire journey.

There were seasons where even brushing my teeth felt like climbing a mountain, where the executive dysfunction was so real, I'd stare at a to-do list until it blurred into oblivion. But I also learned that **small, aligned actions have power**, even on the hardest days.

Sometimes it was as simple as putting on real clothes, not just clean pyjamas, taking the dog out for a walk, eating something nourishing or reaching out to someone I trusted. Those actions may have looked small on the outside, but they sent a powerful message to my brain and body: *I matter. I am worth showing up for.*

And the ripple effect? It was real.

I'd start with a 5-minute gratitude moment and end up handling a difficult task I'd been avoiding for weeks. I'd clean one drawer and feel inspired to clear out my closet. One tiny win would lead to another, and slowly, the fog would lift.

Here's a valuable lesson I've learned and now embody: embracing *nonlinear* progress means recognizing how deeply interconnected everything is. When you take one loving action, it doesn't stay in one part of your life. It spreads. It touches your relationships, your energy, and your belief in yourself. That's what makes small actions so sacred. It's never just about that moment. It's about who you become when you keep choosing yourself, one brave step at a time.

You are doing the sacred work of remembering who you are. You are stripping away the lies, standing face-to-face with your fears, and rooting yourself in your worth. Now is the time to take action. This is your moment, not tomorrow, not someday, *now.*

This is the moment you stop waiting, for clarity, for confidence, for permission, and start moving, not perfectly but bravely, not with certainty but with self-trust. Because transformation doesn't come from knowing what to do. It comes from doing it, one small, self-honoring step at a time, even when fear is loud, even when the path is messy.

Let this be the chapter where you rise, not because you have all the answers but because you finally understand the truth: **you don't need to earn your worth to begin.** You never did. You are not starting from broken. You are rising from *becoming.* And now, you're ready, not just to think about change but to *embody it.* You've created the vision. You've dared to imagine what life could look like without the old scripts, the protective patterns, and the limiting beliefs that once kept you stuck.

Now comes the part that separates daydreams from transformation: You have to **move into alignment with it.** You have to start to **embody it.**

This is the step where vision becomes movement, where the future you've imagined stops living in your mind and starts showing up in your body, your choices, your energy, and your voice. Because change doesn't happen through insight alone. It happens through integration.

You're not just thinking different thoughts. You're practicing being the version of you who *already lives* the vision, the one who breathes like she belongs, who walks like she trusts herself, and who speaks like she knows she's worthy. Not someday. **Now.** This is the moment when transformation stops being conceptual and becomes *cellular.* Because once your body believes it, your life begins to reflect it.

Embodiment Is the Bridge

Here's what most people miss: limiting beliefs don't just live in the mind. They are stored in the body, etched into your posture, your breathing, your nervous system. Your subconscious doesn't just think in thoughts. It speaks through sensation. That's why you can feel clear, inspired, and ready... and still find yourself procrastinating, shrinking, over-controlling, or quitting before you really begin.

If your nervous system still perceives change as a threat, it will quietly pull you back into the familiar, not because you're lazy, broken, or unmotivated, but because **your body doesn't feel safe yet in the new story.**

This is why alignment isn't just mental, it's *physiological.*

Self-Honoring Action

Moving into alignment means moving *with* your nervous system, not against it. It means learning the language of your body—tightness, fatigue, hesitation, overwhelm—and responding with presence instead of pressure, compassion instead of control, curiosity instead of criticism. Because your nervous system isn't the problem. It's your guide. It's brilliant. It's been working to protect you all along, sending signals to let you know where healing is needed and where safety must be rebuilt.

And when you begin to understand its cues and create space for regulation, you stop seeing your reactions as resistance and start seeing them as **requests for care, attention, and safety.**

This is where *regulation becomes your superpower*, not to push harder but to create the internal conditions required for your new identity to take root.

This Is the Shift

This is the step where you stop *holding* the vision and start *living* it, moment by moment, choice by choice, breath by breath. Because alignment isn't a leap. It's a *practice.* And when you practice it with intention (next chapter) and compassion, you stop waiting for the life you want and start embodying the one you were born for.

To embody your vision means to *live* it now, not someday when it's all figured out, but today in the way you breathe, speak, move, and choose. It means aligning your habits, thoughts, energy, and presence with the version of you who already has what you're creating. You're not just visualizing a future self. You're rehearsing her in real time.

You're wiring in her patterns, her posture, and her presence, not perfectly but consistently.

This is how vision becomes movement.

This Is What Embodiment Looks Like in My Life

Embodying my vision isn't always graceful. It's not about perfection. It's about choosing to *show up*, especially when every old belief is trying to talk me out of it.

I'm building a life as an author, a keynote speaker, a public figure, someone who stands on stages and writes words that change lives. But make no mistake, the patterns I've worked to rewrite still try to whisper, *"Who do you think you are?"* They tell me it's safer to stay small, to avoid the spotlight to protect myself from failure, from judgment, from being seen.

In those exact moments, I pause. I *check in with my nervous system*, my ultimate guiding system. If I feel tension, hesitation, or overwhelm, I don't see that as failure. I see it as **feedback**. I ask, *What story is trying to take over right now?* I name it. I challenge it. And I remind myself of the truth:

I am worthy of this vision. I don't need to earn it or prove it. I just need to honor it through action.

So I take the step. I write the chapter. I say yes to the thing that scares me. I walk into the room with shoulders back and heart open, not because the fear is gone but because I refuse to let it take the lead anymore. When doubt creeps in, I ask myself, *"What would Bestselling Author Monic think, feel, or choose in this moment? How would she show up?"* And then I align. I align my thoughts. I align my choices. I align my behavior, not with who I was… but with who I'm becoming.

That is embodiment. It's the daily, courageous decision to move in sync with your vision, not your fear. You let your future self take the lead even when your past self wants to take the wheel.

And if I can do it, so can you. This is your opportunity to practice showing up differently. You double down not out of pressure or perfectionism but from a place of power. You engage with the take-away reflections in this book. You dive deep into the practical tools I've given you. You follow through with the journaling prompts, not because you're trying to prove anything but because you've made a decision: **to honor this process, to honor your vision, and to honor *yourself*.** This is where the shift happens, not when it's easy and not when it's perfect but when it's *real*. And right now, this is as real as it gets.

This is your becoming. Claim it. Live it. Love it. Let's move from reading to becoming. Take out your workbook.

CHAPTER 14

B.E.C.O.M.I.N.G.

Integrate with Intention

> "Insight opens the door. Embodiment walks you through it."
>
> — Monic Ayotte

Where Insight Becomes Identity

In the last chapter, you began *Moving into Alignment.* You created the vision. You started taking action. You said yes to the version of yourself you're becoming. That was your turning point, the moment you stopped just imagining what's possible and started walking toward it. That was the *activation.*

But this? **This is the integration**, because starting is one thing. *Staying* with it is another. You've felt the spark. Now it's time to tend the flame.

Alignment is when you *initiate* the shift, when you align your choices with your vision and begin stepping into the new self. Integration is when you stay in that alignment long enough for it to become your new normal.

This is the part where transformation becomes *durable*, where healing moves from "breakthrough" to *embodied identity*, where you don't just say and do the right things, you *live* them, where you don't just take bold steps, you *keep* taking them because that is who you are becoming.

Why Integration Matters

Here's what I've seen time and time again with clients who reach this stage of the journey, **the integration** phase. It is where the shift starts to feel real, not because of a single breakthrough but because of the *compound effect* of the steady momentum created by the steps that came before. They've done the work. They've envisioned what's possible. They've taken aligned action. And now, life begins to reflect it.

Things shift. It's inevitable. Relationships feel different. The noise of old patterns starts to quiet. There's more clarity, more focus, more presence.

They begin to see the truth more clearly, not the conditioned filters of fear or doubt but what's *actually* true. They find themselves less distracted by old stories and more anchored in their purpose. It's beautiful to witness. But here's what's also true: **clarity can feel disorienting when you're not used to it.**

Because when you start to move differently, your nervous system notices. When you start speaking up, slowing down, setting boundaries, and choosing what honors you, your old programming doesn't always applaud. It resists. It warns. It pulls. You're stepping into unfamiliar territory. You're choosing change. And the mind, wired for familiarity, may try to convince you to turn back.

Most of the time this phase feels like freedom: expansive, electric, energizing. But sometimes it feels messy and uncertain. That's the *debris* of the old life still floating to the surface. And this is where many people are tempted to retreat, not because they're failing but because they're *feeling*. They confuse discomfort with misdirection. They interpret doubt as a sign to stop. They want to go back, not because it was better but because it was known.

Don't let that be you.

You are not lost. You are not doing it wrong. You are in the middle of **becoming.**

This is the moment where real change begins to settle, not in your mind but in your body, your habits, your nervous system, your *life.* And I promise you this: if you keep showing up with presence, with intention, and with even the smallest daily acts of alignment, you will keep experiencing growth and expansion. Let this be the moment you trust the process. Let this be the moment you trust *yourself.*

What Integration Really Looks Like

Integration isn't about doing more. It's about living differently. It's honoring the new beliefs in real-time moments:

Saying *no* when your old self would've said yes to avoid discomfort.

Breathing through anxiety instead of performing your way through it.

Holding boundaries instead of explaining them to death.

Choosing rest without guilt.

Speaking from truth instead of shrinking to be liked.

It's choosing from your *becoming,* not from your past.

And it's **not** about being perfect. It's about being present and showing up to your own life with consistency, compassion, and clarity even when it's uncomfortable, *especially* when it's uncomfortable.

Your Nervous System Is the Gatekeeper

This step and the following one are deeply embodied. Awareness and mindfulness are no longer just practices, they're becoming part of who you are. They're not something you occasionally reach for; they're becoming your default way of moving through the world. And that is the most important shift of all.

When presence becomes your baseline, everything else begins to shift with more ease. Your choices, your boundaries, your energy, they begin to align, not through force but through flow. Why? Because you're no longer operating from survival. You're leading from awareness. But here's what you need to know: even now, your nervous system is still doing its job. It's scanning for danger, assessing risk, looking for signs that say, *"This isn't safe,"* not because you're broken but because you're human.

If boldness, visibility, or taking up space felt unsafe in the past, your body may still try to pull you back into old patterns of protection, not with loud alarms but with quiet signals: fatigue, hesitation, tension, or procrastination.

That's not failure. That's feedback.

Integration isn't about pushing through those cues. It's about working *with* your body, not against it. It's about noticing those moments with compassion, pausing with intention, and asking *"What's happening here?"* instead of *"What's wrong with me?"* And then gently reminding yourself:

"I'm safe to be here now." "This is new, not dangerous." "My nervous system is catching up to the new me."

Because the moment your body begins to feel safe, your new identity becomes available, not just in your thoughts but in your tone, your posture, your pace, and your presence. It starts to live in *how* you show up, not just *who* you're becoming.

The Power of Consistency

Let me tell you, consistency is challenging when you live with ADHD. It's not about laziness or lack of willpower. It's about having a brain that craves novelty, struggles with structure, and loses track of time like it's a magic trick. And yes... squirrel...

For a long time, I beat myself up for being "inconsistent." I'd start strong, feel amazing, and then completely lose steam. I internalized it as failure. But it wasn't failure; it was *wiring.* What I needed wasn't more discipline. What I needed was more compassion and a new definition of consistency. Consistency doesn't mean perfection. It doesn't mean doing the same thing at the same time every day with military precision. It means *coming back to yourself,* again and again. It means picking up where you left off without shame. It means finding rhythms that work for *your* brain, not someone else's.

For me, that meant building rituals, not routines. It meant forgiving myself for the messy days and celebrating the wins, no matter how small. It meant learning that micro-actions count, especially when your brain is already juggling a thousand tabs. Consistency, for me, became an act of radical self-trust. Not rigid. Not punitive. But rooted in this question: "*What's the most loving thing I can do for myself today?*" And doing that, over and over again, became my definition of success.

So, if you're still wondering about the difference between the last step, **Movement**, and this one, **Integration**, think of it like trying out a new mattress or a new couch. At first, it feels unfamiliar. It shifts the space. It changes the way you move, rest, and experience your environment. You might question if it was the right choice.

But over time, with each use, you begin to settle into it. You remember *why* you made the change in the first place, because the old one no longer supported you or wasn't the right fit. And as you keep showing up for the decision you made, it becomes your new normal. It stops feeling different and starts feeling like *you*.

That's integration. It's the space where the new you isn't just something you try on. It's who you come home to.

CHAPTER 15

B.E.C.O.M.I.N.G.

Nurture Your Becoming, The Momentum Reclaim

> "Momentum doesn't mean you never slow down.
> It means you know how to rise again wiser, softer, stronger."
>
> — Monic Ayotte

There comes a point in every transformation where the energy dips. The high of the breakthrough wears off. The clarity blurs. The spark flickers. You've done so much, envisioned, aligned, integrated and then… life happens. Old patterns knock. Stress creeps in. Motivation wavers.

And it's in this space, the in-between, where most people begin to doubt. Or they drift from the awareness they've worked so hard to build, stepping away from their internal guidance system, not because they've failed but because life got loud. Urgent. Sometimes unbearably painful. Maybe it was a crisis. Maybe it was cancer. Maybe it was simply survival.

But this is also where we're called to face a deeper truth:

If we've lost our footing, it's not just because life pulled us away. It's because we drifted from our core values. We stopped embodying the version of ourselves we were becoming, not out of weakness but out of old wiring, out of protection, out of forgetting. And now, we remember. Now, we return.

And 2023 was my reminder. It was a season that stripped everything back and made me face what I hadn't yet fully realized. **I had underestimated the need to nurture my becoming,** not because I didn't care, not because I wasn't committed, but because I didn't yet understand just how vital this step was—*What it really meant* to sustain growth in the middle of life's messiness. I thought momentum meant movement, consistency, and drive. But then came the storm.

My energy was consumed by caregiving, crisis, and survival. I was navigating the emotional weight of watching someone I love suffer through cancer. And in the process, I stopped tending to myself. I drifted not out of failure, but out of perceived necessity. I did what so many of us do when life gets loud. I put my *becoming* on pause and shifted into protection mode.

And here's what I learned: Even with all my tools, all my awareness, all my growth... I could still forget. I could still lose my footing. I stepped away from the practices that anchored me. I disconnected from the values that once lit my path. I slowly stopped embodying the version of myself I had worked so hard to become, not because I gave up but because I didn't yet understand that **nurturing your becoming isn't optional. It's essential.** It's not something you do *after* the chaos. It's something you build into the rhythm of your life, *especially* when things feel chaotic.

And so, I began the work of returning, gently and without shame. I reminded myself that growth is not erased in the pause. It's strengthened by the way we choose to rise again. This is what *Momentum Reclaim* is about. It's not about forcing your way back. It's about remembering your way forward. It's about nourishing the root of who you are becoming, even when the world feels like it's demanding everything else from you. Because losing your footing doesn't mean you've lost your path. It means you're human. And the most powerful thing you can do is *return*, with more compassion, more wisdom, and more devotion than ever before.

What Is Momentum Reclaim?

Momentum Reclaim is not about pushing harder. It's not about hustle, grind, or getting back "on track" as fast as possible. It's about choosing to reconnect, to re-engage, and to nurture your process with care, not criticism. It's about remembering that growth is not linear. It's layered. There are dips. Pauses. Spirals. Repeats.

Momentum Reclaim is the practice of returning to yourself in those moments. It's the art of coming back after a stall, not with shame but with self-trust. It's knowing how to keep your *becoming* alive, even when life feels heavy or unclear. And for me, it was this very practice, this quiet, persistent act of returning that brought me to one of the most powerful realizations of my life: I had barely scratched the surface of what it meant to *nurture* my becoming.

Now I am inspired beyond anything I've ever felt before to meet myself with a new level of devotion, to tend to my becoming with next-level love, with fierce compassion, and with the kind of care I once reserved only for others. Because the greatest transformation isn't found in the moments when everything is going right. It's found in the moments when you lose your way and *choose* to come back anyway.

This step teaches you how to stay with yourself, not just when it's exciting but when it's uncomfortable, I mean deeply uncomfortable. When your nervous system is tired. When your thoughts start recycling old doubts. When nothing seems to be "working," and yet you choose to keep showing up. Because the difference between those who transform and those who don't? It's not willpower. It's not discipline. It's the ability to *reclaim the moment.* It's the ability to say:

> *"I may have paused—but I am not done."*
>
> *"I may have forgotten—but I can remember."*
>
> *"I may have slipped—but I can rise with wisdom I didn't have before."*

This is what it means to nurture your becoming, gently, consistently, and without panic when the flames flicker.

Your Growth Is Not Erased

One of the greatest lies we carry is that a setback cancels our progress, that if we lose momentum, we go back to zero. But growth doesn't work like that.

Every insight you've had... Every truth you've uncovered... Every shift you've made... It's still yours.

Even when you stall, it's still alive inside you. The work now is to **reclaim it**, not from pressure but from devotion.

How to Reclaim Momentum With Grace

Reclaiming momentum doesn't mean forcing yourself to "get back on track." It means asking:

- *What brings me back to myself when I feel off-center?*
- *What helps me reconnect to my why?*
- *What can I do today not perfectly but intentionally to move with purpose again?*

Sometimes the answer is movement. Sometimes it's stillness. Sometimes it's reaching out. Sometimes it's going inward. But always, it starts with one small step, one aligned choice, one breath of self-compassion.

Practice the Return

The ones who go the distance are not the ones who never fall. They're the ones who *always come back.* They don't let the stall become a stop. They don't make failure mean something about their worth. They just... begin again. So have I. And so will you. This is the moment to forgive, and learn from the slips, celebrate the return, and honor the rhythm of your becoming.

So come back to the truth that lit you up. Re-read the words you underlined. Revisit the promise you made to yourself. Reconnect to the vision that stirred your soul. Don't check out. Lean in. This isn't a breakdown; it's a breakthrough asking for a breath. You're not broken. You're becoming. You're allowed to pause, but not to quit.

This is about heart, commitment, and devotion to yourself. You are not starting over. You are *stepping back in.* Let this moment not be the end of your fire but the fanning of your flame.

Your *Momentum Reclaim* Ritual

When the spark fades... reclaim it. Here's how:

1. **Pause.** Breathe. Meet yourself here in the pain, the fear, the confusion, and the sadness.
2. **Name what pulled you off track.** Fear? Exhaustion? Distraction? A familiar emotional loop?
3. **Ask:** *"What does my becoming need of me need right now? What does it want for me?"*
4. **Reaffirm your choice.** Write it. Say it. Feel it in your bones. *"I'm not starting over. I'm stepping back in."*
5. **Take one aligned action.** It doesn't need to be grand or flashy, but it needs to be *honest.*

One page. One walk. One choice. That's how momentum lives again. This is your moment. You've got this! Now we move into the workbook.

CHAPTER 16

B.E.C.O.M.I.N.G.

Ground in Your Identity

> "We do not learn from experience… we learn from reflecting on experience."
>
> —John Dewey

You've done the work. You've named the beliefs. You've felt the fear. You've moved into alignment. You've integrated, returned, and reclaimed. You've walked through each step of your becoming with courage, honesty, and intention.

And now… now you root. Now you stop reaching for who you're becoming… and start *being* her. This is the step where you stabilize the identity you've been building, emotionally, energetically, and neurologically. It's where the shift becomes your new standard. It's no longer a stretch to show up as your highest self. It's your baseline.

You're not surprised by your alignment anymore. You *expect it.* You don't perform confidence. You *embody* it. You don't try to prove your worth. You *radiate* it.

Because now, you are not just changing, you are *changed.*

What Grounding Really Means

To ground in your identity means to plant both feet firmly in who you've become. It's no longer a future you reach for; it's the *home* you keep returning to. Grounding isn't about striving. It's about settling in. It's about allowing this version of you to become so familiar, so integrated, that you no longer question whether it's real. It just fits.

You're no longer rehearsing your worthiness.

You're no longer negotiating your boundaries.

You're no longer wondering if you're "doing it right."

You're just *being.* You speak from truth. You rest without guilt. You say yes with power and no with peace.

The Moment You Know It's Real

This is the moment when success doesn't feel like pressure; it feels like flow. This is the moment when softness doesn't feel like weakness; it feels like strength. This is the moment when power doesn't feel performative; it feels like *you.*

Your nervous system no longer panics at visibility or change. It recognizes safety as your new normal. Your identity is no longer half-in, half-out. It's *anchored.* You don't need external validation. You carry your own knowing. This is the step where people around you start to say,

"There's something different about you."

But the truth is, it's not that you've changed overnight. It's that you've *come home* to who you always were beneath the layers.

The Power of Being

Let's be clear: this isn't about perfection. It's about *presence.* It's about walking into the world with both feet grounded in your truth, no longer wobbling between the old and the new. You no longer need to "try" to be her. You *are* her. She's how you respond, how you walk into a room, how you rest, how you rise, and how you lead. This isn't about becoming anymore. This is about being. Not as a performance. Not as a mask. But as your most rooted, integrated, unapologetic self.

And From Here? You live it. You let the vision live through you. You speak the truth you once feared. You hold the boundaries you once wavered on. You soften without shrinking. You rise without apologizing. You live from wholeness, not because you've arrived at some finish line but because you now know that you never needed to earn your worth. You only needed to remember it.

Stillness? Stillness is where the soul speaks. It's where the truth rises to the surface. And it's where transformation truly roots itself. Because contrary to popular belief, **progress isn't always found in forward motion**. Sometimes, the most powerful momentum happens in the stillness, the sacred pause, the brave, intentional breath when you stop, turn inward, and say to yourself with wonder, *"Holy crap! Look how far I've come."*

Growth isn't just about the work you do. It's about the way you *see* the work you've already done.

It's one thing to keep striving. It's another to pause, look in the mirror of your life, and softly say, *"I'm not who I used to be."* There's a sacred power in the pause. It's the moment when we step off the treadmill of self-improvement and say, *"Hold on... Let me see how far I've come."*

Too often, we evaluate our lives with a harsh lens. We focus on what still isn't done, how far we still have to go, or all the ways we think we're still falling short. But real transformation, the kind that rewires your brain and redefines your future, asks you to shift that lens.

It asks you to look through the eyes of love, to be your own cheerleader, and to notice the quiet progress, the subtle shifts, and the victories no one else sees but you feel deep in your bones.

Here's what I've learned, not just from decades of deep self-exploration and healing but from sitting across from countless souls as a psychotherapist and hypnotist: this step right here, evaluating your progress through a loving, compassionate lens, is one of the most overlooked (and dare I say underrated?) parts of the growth process. And it's not because we're lazy or unaware or not doing "enough." Quite the opposite. My clients are some of the most hardworking, heart-centered, soul-searching humans you'll ever meet. But when it comes to *pausing* to honor their progress? When it comes to *celebrating* how far they've come? Suddenly... the resistance shows up.

There's a quiet discomfort. A hesitation. A shrinking back. And more often than not, they say something like:

- *"It feels weird to praise myself."*
- *"Isn't that arrogant?"*
- *"What if I get too confident and then mess up?"*
- *"It feels selfish to focus on me like that."*

Sound familiar?

Here's the truth: **that hesitation is not a personal flaw. It's a limiting belief.** Yes, even in this step is part of the programming we're here to dismantle.

Many of us were taught, directly or indirectly, that humility meant downplaying our wins and that celebrating ourselves made us self-absorbed, full of ego, or somehow "too much." Somewhere along the way, we absorbed the belief that if we acknowledged our growth, we were being boastful or inviting failure. But let me say this loud and clear: acknowledging your growth is not arrogance; it's alignment. Celebrating your progress is not vanity; it's *validation*. It's how you rewire your brain to believe that change is not only possible, it's *already happening.*

If your inner voice resists this, that's okay. That's just more evidence of the work. That voice that tells you to shrink back when you want to celebrate? That's your old programming trying to protect you in the only way it knows how. So let's offer it some love, and then let's gently challenge it.

Because if we don't learn to witness, track, and celebrate the moments of growth, those moments pass us by like milestones we never noticed.

And what a tragedy that would be, to become someone new and not even realize it.

This reflection, this celebration—it's not optional. **It's a *crucial* part of breaking through limiting beliefs.** Because when you see yourself clearly, when you witness the change and name it and feel it, you reinforce the truth:

I am changing. I am growing. I am no longer who I used to be.

That truth, when embodied, dismantles old stories at their root.

So if this step feels hard, you're not alone. You're not broken. You're just bumping up against an old belief that says, "I'm not supposed to be proud of myself." Let's rewrite that right now:

You are allowed to be proud. You are allowed to celebrate. You are allowed to feel joy about your progress without guilt. You are allowed to shine. And if it feels unfamiliar, if it feels uncomfortable, that's okay. That just means you're growing into a version of yourself who knows how to celebrate without apology.

And trust me... *You? You are* powerful beyond measure.

The Science Behind It

Let's get nerdy for a second.

Your brain is a meaning-making machine. It's constantly scanning your environment and your experiences to determine: *What's important? What should I remember? What should I repeat?*

And the answer is: **whatever gets rewarded**.

So what happens to our brain when we celebrate a win? When you acknowledge a win, no matter how small, you trigger your brain's reward circuitry. Dopamine is released. This "feel-good" chemical tells your nervous system, "Yes! That was freakin' fantastic! Let's do it again."

So when you reflect on your progress, when you celebrate a win (even silently in your journal during your gratitude moment), your brain responds by reinforcing the new neural pathways you're building. It's a beautiful feedback loop:

Action ➔ Evaluation ➔ Celebration ➔ Rewiring ➔ More Empowered Action

If you ignore the progress… If you say, *"It's not good enough yet,"* then your brain doesn't register it. And your old default settings? They remain stronger. Here is an interesting truth: What we celebrate gets reinforced. You are teaching your brain a new way of being. And that requires moments of reflection, of reverence, of celebration (remember mindfulness? creating that space?). This is where confidence is born, not from perfection but from tracking and celebrating growth.

Every time you choose to respond instead of react… Every time you questioned a thought that used to run your life… Every time you stood in your truth instead of your fear… That's progress. That's evidence. That's a win.

Let's not sugarcoat it: **the inner work you're doing takes courage and commitment**. It's not flashy. It's not loud. You don't get a trophy or standing ovation for it (even though you deserve one). But make no mistake, it is sacred. It is soul-deep. And it is life-changing.

When you give yourself the grace to pause and reflect, to truly witness the ways you've shifted, grown, softened, or strengthened, you give your transformation the validation it deserves. Self-reflection is not a break *from* the work. It *is* the work. It's not wasted time. It's sacred space. It's your emotional and spiritual GPS recalibrating. It's how you track the invisible progress your heart is making and the shifts in your beliefs, your choices, and your inner dialogue. And these shifts? They are everything. You begin to notice:

- You don't spiral when things go wrong like you used to.
- You say "no" without apology.
- You pause before reacting.
- You reach for compassion instead of criticism.
- You dare to believe that maybe, just maybe, *you're enough.*

Let me be clear: these are not small wins. These are **monumental shifts in identity**, in belief, in the way you relate to yourself and the world. These are the fruits of the deep, inner rewiring that only happens when you've been brave enough to face your limiting beliefs head-on. And that's why this chapter matters so much.

When you're in the thick of transformation, it can be hard to see the change. You're so close to it. It's like watching grass grow, until one day you step back and realize you're standing in a blooming field you planted with your bare hands. **That's what reflection does.** It zooms you out just enough to see the beauty of what's unfolding. It helps you track the wins you might otherwise miss. And yes, it also shows you where you've stalled, where old beliefs are creeping back in, and where your fear might be masquerading as logic. That's not failure. That's feedback.

So if you've felt stuck lately, uninspired, or like nothing's "working," pause and reflect. Chances are, your breakthrough isn't ahead of you. It's already happening… and it just needs your recognition to rise fully to the surface.

Celebrate Every Win! Yes, Even the Tiny Ones

We have a tendency to breeze right past our victories, don't we? We rush on to the next thing and move the finish line the moment we get close. We shrug off our success with a casual, "Oh, that was nothing," as if acknowledging it somehow cheapens it.

But let me remind you of a powerful truth: **what you celebrate, expands.** Your nervous system is listening. Your subconscious is watching. Every time you celebrate yourself, you reinforce the belief that *you are worthy* of success, of progress, of joy.

And if I sound like a broken record right now? **Good. That means it's sinking in. That means you're waking up to the truth of who you really are and how powerful you are.** And that, my friend, is worth repeating. Write it down. Say it out loud. Light a candle. Do a happy dance in your kitchen. Because the more you honor these moments, the more your brain learns: *"This matters. Let's do more of it."*

Learn from Setbacks Without Shaming Yourself

Let's clear this up once and for all: **progress is not linear**. It's not a staircase. It's a wild, twisty, glorious, unpredictable dance. And sometimes you trip. You fall back into an old belief. You make a choice you swore you'd outgrown. And guess what? That doesn't mean you're broken or that you're a failure. It means, "Congratulations! You're human."

When setbacks happen, and they will, don't go into shame mode. Go into **curiosity mode**. Ask yourself:

- What did this challenge teach me about my old wiring?
- How did I respond differently than I would have a year ago?
- Where can I show myself compassion in this moment?

When you reflect with love instead of judgment, every so-called "failure" becomes a step forward. **Shame keeps you stuck. Awareness sets you free.**

Awareness: The Silent Witness of Your Becoming

This is where the magic deepens: **awareness**. Awareness is your inner witness, your soul's gentle spotlight. It sees what the world can't yet see. It notices the micro-shifts and the micro-moments of awakening. These moments may be quiet, but trust me, they are **loud with transformation**. And awareness helps you catch them before they pass by unnoticed. So ask yourself:

- Where am I showing up more authentically?
- What thoughts feel new, freer, more empowering?
- What patterns have loosened their grip?
- What am I proud of right now?

I promise you, if you've made it this far in this book, you are not the same person who picked it up. You *can't* be. It's impossible. Something inside you has shifted, subtly, powerfully, undeniably. Because you've done more than read words on a page. You've questioned old beliefs.

You've peeled back layers that no longer serve you. You've said yes to seeing yourself more clearly, more honestly, more lovingly.

And that? That's *becoming.*

Change doesn't always arrive with fireworks. Sometimes it tiptoes in, soft and steady, through your quiet decisions, your brave reflections, your willingness to stay with yourself instead of abandoning who you are. But make no mistake: change has already taken root. Growth and rising are in motion. The old stories are loosening their grip, and something *truer* is rising in their place.

And awareness? Awareness is your sacred mirror. It reflects back to you not who you've been, but who you're becoming. So pause. Look. *See yourself,* not with judgment, not with comparison, but with love and admiration. Because this version of you? It is blooming. It is shifting, transforming, and expanding. And it's just getting started!

Make This Your New Rhythm, Your New Lifestyle

This isn't a one-time exercise or practice. This is a rhythm, a lifestyle of reflection and celebration. Let it anchor your transformation.

- **Reflect weekly or monthly.** Don't just move on, pause.
- **Celebrate ALL of the wins.** They are your new foundation.
- **Learn with love.** Let every misstep become a message.
- **Stay aware.** Let your inner witness keep you aligned.

Because when you regularly evaluate your progress, you don't just stay on the path, you **own** it. You **embody** it. You **lead** yourself with purpose and grace. And friend, let me remind you of this sacred truth: You are doing better than you think. I guarantee it! The fact that you're here, still reading, still trying, still choosing growth, that alone is a HUGE WIN. Keep going. Keep believing. Keep *becoming.*

Your transformation is happening. It's not some distant horizon you're chasing. It's **happening right now**, one breath, one reflection, one shift at a time.

I celebrate you! xo

You have walked through every step of the formula. And here is the true gift:

You never outgrow it.

You carry it.

You return to it when life stretches you.

You lean on it when doubt creeps in.

You deepen it as you rise.

This is no longer a method you're learning.

It is a tool you own.

A framework that meets you at every new edge of growth.

This isn't the end of the work.

It's the beginning of mastery.

And mastery isn't perfection.

It's remembering, again and again, who you are becoming.

CHAPTER 17

Self-Love

Your Own Love Story—By You, For You

"Owning our story and loving ourselves through that process is the bravest thing that we'll ever do."

—Brené Brown

You've walked through B.E.C.O.M.I.N.G.

The foundation is yours.

What comes next is an intentional addition.

Not because you're lacking anything.

But because growth is generous.

The next chapter is here to support you in integrating this work even more deeply into your life.

Receive it as something extra.

Something supportive.

Something you choose.

There was a time when self-love felt like a foreign language, something I admired in others, maybe even studied, but couldn't quite speak for myself. I'd repeat the affirmations. I'd read the books. I'd talk about healing and worth and self-compassion. But deep down, there was a hollow place inside of me that wasn't convinced.

Because the truth is, I didn't just lack self-love, I was afraid of it—afraid of what it would mean to truly choose myself, to stop proving, punishing, or pleasing, and to stop needing someone else to validate my worth. I had built an identity around control, perfectionism, and chasing approval… and beneath it all lived a quiet, persistent belief: *I am not lovable as I am.*

That belief shaped everything. It drove me into war with my own body, where anorexia, bulimia, and body dysmorphia ruled my every thought. I starved myself to feel worthy. I binged to fill the void. I punished myself through deprivation and obsession, thinking that maybe if I got small enough, thin enough, or perfect enough that I'd finally be enough.

But that moment never came. Because no matter how much I shrank, no matter how hard I tried, it was never enough to quiet the ache that lived inside, the ache of believing I had to earn love through suffering.

That same belief echoed through every relationship I entered. I attracted toxicity like a magnet, poured myself into people who gave me crumbs, and feared boundaries like they were weapons instead of lifelines. I over-gave, over-functioned, and disappeared into the needs of others, desperate to feel chosen. And yet, with every act of self-abandonment, I moved further and further away from myself. And through all of that, something in me never gave up. Some deeper, wiser part of me was still searching, still hoping, still *trying* to come home to myself.

Let's get one thing straight: self-love is not about thinking you're perfect. It's not about standing in the mirror with forced affirmations or pretending everything's okay. Self-love is about *truth.* It's about becoming your own safe place, your own sanctuary. It's about looking yourself in the eyes and saying, "Even here, even now, I choose you." It's the moment you stop abandoning yourself to be loved by someone else. It's the moment you decide that your voice, your needs, your rest, your healing, *all of it* matters.

And you know what? I thought I had come to understand this pretty clearly as I have been doing this work for decades, and I've heard the concept of self-love explained in so many beautiful ways. But the most powerful, soul-shaking description I've ever heard came from Kathleen Cameron.

I was listening to her speak about self-love, but this time? I received what I was hearing differently. She began by talking about her daughters, the deep, all-consuming, unconditional love she feels for them. The kind of love that shows up through presence, protection, pride, and unwavering support. Then she said something that brought tears streaming down my face.

She shared how she gives herself that same love, every single minute of every day. That same level of devotion, tenderness, loyalty and unconditional support, she gives it to herself. At that moment, I *got it.* I didn't just understand self-love, I *felt* it more deeply, more powerfully than I ever had before. What a gift.

I realized that as far as I've come, I'm still learning to love myself at *that* level, still learning to be my own soft place to land, and still learning to give myself the kind of love I've spent so long offering to everyone else. Challenge accepted. Because there is no goal more sacred.

Self-love isn't about ego or perfection. It's not about standing in front of the mirror and pretending to adore your reflection. It's not about doing everything right. Self-love is about *truth.* It's the quiet, steady decision to stop abandoning yourself for approval and to start honoring who you are: messy, beautiful, and still *becoming.*

It's the voice that says: *I matter.* It's the pause before you say yes to something that drains you. It's the hand you place over your heart when the old stories rise. It's the whispered reminder: "*You're allowed to be here. You're allowed to take up space. You're allowed to rest.*"

But to love yourself, you have to face the beliefs that tell you you're not worthy of it and the lies that say you have to earn love, perform for it, or punish yourself into it. These aren't just thoughts, they're echoes of wounds, stories written long ago in places where you weren't seen, or were only valued when you were small, silent, or selfless.

And those beliefs? They show up in the most subtle ways. They tell you not to eat when you're hungry. They make you apologize for having needs. They keep you in relationships that deplete you. They convince you that boundaries are selfish, that rest is laziness, and that self-celebration is arrogance.

But here's the truth: *You don't have to earn your way back to love. You just have to remember it's already yours.*

Self-love grows in small, sacred moments: the ones where you catch the lie and gently replace it with truth, the ones where you give yourself grace instead of judgment, and the ones where you make different choices, not because you have it all figured out but because you're done living like you don't matter.

It grows through awareness, when you finally start to hear the inner critic for what it is: an old voice, not your truth. It grows through compassion, when you hold space for your pain without needing to fix it right away. It grows through boundaries, when you stop letting people walk through your soul with muddy feet and start choosing peace over people-pleasing. And it grows through practice. You won't believe the new story at first. But if you keep speaking it, writing it, and living it, it will become your new truth.

The girl I once was, the one who starved herself, hated her body, feared her voice, and didn't believe this life was possible, she didn't think she'd ever feel free. But I look at her now with so much love, because *she got me here.* And now, it's your turn.

It's your turn to stop shrinking for love that doesn't require your disappearance. It's your turn to stop waiting for someone else to tell you you're enough. It's your turn to stop chasing worthiness and start *claiming* it. You don't have to be anyone else. You don't have to wait until you're "fixed." You are already worthy, already whole, and already lovable. So begin, right here, exactly as you are. Begin again and again if you have to—but begin. Because the moment you stop abandoning yourself, your entire life begins to change.

And you? You are worth every single step of this journey, not the polished version, not the highlight reel, and not the one you show the world when you've got your armor on and your smile fixed in place. I'm talking about this version of you, right here, right now. The one who is still tender in places, still figuring things out, still holding the ache of who she used to be in one hand and the hope of who she's *becoming* in the other. Can you look at her not with critique but with reverence? With awe? With kindness?

Because this moment, this breath, this quiet reckoning, is where true transformation takes root, not in some far-off destination called "enough," not in a list of completed goals or a perfectly healed inner child, but here, in the gentle, sacred decision to love yourself exactly as you are, not someday...now.

Self-love isn't the dessert at the end of your healing. It's the soil everything grows from. It's the foundation under your feet. It's the steady pulse beneath every choice you make. And without it, all the awareness, action, and surrender in the world will feel like you're still trying to earn something. But with it? With true, embodied, unconditional self-love? You become unshakable.

I don't mean the kind of love that lives on bathroom mirror sticky notes or comes packaged in pretty Instagram quotes, though those can be lovely. I mean the kind of self-love that meets you when you're falling apart, the kind that sits with you in the silence, the kind that doesn't flinch when you're sobbing in your car or questioning everything you thought you knew, the kind that says, "You are safe with me now."

By now you know that for decades, I lacked the ability, the permission, to love myself that way. My inner voice was sharp, demanding, and relentlessly focused on what needed fixing. Even after years of deep inner work, I'd still catch myself measuring my worth in milestones, progress, productivity, and how much I'd accomplished. I wasn't nurturing myself the way true self-love would, but I was managing myself, treating my healing like a to-do list instead of a relationship.

So in 2023 when I stepped into the caregiver role, it was humbling and heart-stretching in ways I couldn't have anticipated. It invited me, no, *demanded* that I pause and check in and slow down long enough to ask myself, with raw honesty: Am I truly living this? Am I loving myself in the chaos, in the fatigue, in the moments that don't look "healed"? Or am I still waiting until everyone else is okay, until I've earned my peace, until I've proved enough?

That season of my life became a wake-up call, a sacred reminder that this path, this journey of wellness and wholeness, isn't linear. It's not a finish line or a box to check. It's not about arrival, but it's about return. It's a deep, ongoing practice of coming home to yourself, again and again, with gentleness and grace. And for that gift of awareness, for the way it pulled me back into presence and truth, I am so incredibly grateful.

That's what I want for you, not as an afterthought, not as an optional extra, but as the whole point. Because when you love yourself truly, radically, and without condition or apology, everything else starts to shift. Your boundaries change. Your energy softens. Your decisions align. You stop striving and start allowing. You stop proving and start becoming.

This is not about perfection. It never was. This is about presence. Permission. Peace. It's about looking at the parts of you that once made you flinch and saying, "I see you. I honor you. I love you." It's about becoming the one who doesn't just survive your story, but who loves the hell out of the person it shaped you into.

So yes, let awareness join you here too. Let it walk beside you, not to judge but to witness, to notice when old self-talk patterns creep in, to pause when your inner critic rises, and to gently shift the narrative. And instead of spiraling into shame or snapping back into old habits, you get to say, "Wait. That's not my truth anymore. I choose love."

Because how you speak to yourself becomes the blueprint for how the world treats you. Because the love you give yourself becomes the foundation for how you show up in every room, every relationship, every decision. And because, my love, you are not a project to be perfected. You are a miracle to be loved.

So today, right now, can you make yourself a vow? Vow not to get it all right, not to be fearless, but simply to stay, to stop abandoning yourself, to meet your own reflection with awe, and to be the one who says, "I love you. I see you. And I will not leave you."

Let this be your homecoming. Stop seeking outside what has always lived within and realize that you were never too much and never not enough. You were just waiting to be claimed.

This isn't the end of your story. It's the beginning of the most powerful love affair of your life. And it starts right here, with you.

CHAPTER 18

Gratitude

Your Superpower

> "You don't practice gratitude to get more. You practice it to remember you already are more than enough."
>
> — Monic Ayotte

Gratitude is often underestimated, brushed off as a feel-good practice or a nice-to-have attitude. But when you're breaking through limiting beliefs, gratitude isn't just nice. It's *essential.* It's not fluff. It's a frequency. A force. A quiet but radical revolution that rewires your mind and reclaims your power.

When you've lived most of your life trapped in narratives like *"I'm not enough," "I'll never get there,"* or *"It's too late for me,"* your brain becomes trained to scan for lack, for what's missing, for what's wrong. That's not a personal failure. It's biology. Your brain's negativity bias evolved to keep you safe. But in healing work, that bias keeps you small. Gratitude is what begins to shift that.

Gratitude is not about pretending everything is perfect. It's about pausing to recognize what *is* already working. It's about planting your feet in the *now* and saying, *"There's beauty here too."* And that shift?

That simple choice to focus on what's good, even in the middle of the storm? That's where the alchemy begins. Because the truth is, you cannot live in fear and gratitude at the same time. You cannot dwell in unworthiness and gratitude at the same time. You cannot simultaneously believe you are behind and be grateful for who you are becoming.

Gratitude isn't about spiritual bypassing. It's about spiritual anchoring. It's not about ignoring your pain. It's about *witnessing your progress.* It's not about denying your desire for more. It's about celebrating the soil you're already growing in.

And when you do that, when you start seeing what's *right* instead of only what needs fixing, you create emotional safety in your body. That safety is what allows the nervous system to relax. And a relaxed nervous system is a *rewire-ready* nervous system. Gratitude softens the grip of the old story. It says to your brain, *"We're safe here. It's okay to want more and love what we already have."*

And here's the beautiful part: This isn't just emotional, it's *biochemical.* When you practice gratitude, your brain releases a cascade of feel-good chemicals like **dopamine**, **serotonin**, and **oxytocin**, the very hormones responsible for boosting mood, increasing motivation, and deepening connection. Even a simple, genuine moment of gratitude can light up your brain's reward pathways, calming the nervous system and creating a sense of emotional safety. In other words, gratitude doesn't just feel good, it literally *rewires your brain to feel better more often.* And what does this mean for those of us who've danced with anxiety or depression? It means everything.

For anxiety, gratitude acts like a counterbalance to the brain's built-in fear response. It gently pulls you out of hypervigilance and future-focused worry and anchors you back into the present moment, where safety and groundedness live. It soothes the nervous system, lowers cortisol levels, and shifts your focus from "what if" to "what is." It helps your body feel less like it's under attack and more like it's at home.

For depression, gratitude can act as a soft but powerful light in what often feels like emotional darkness. Depression tends to narrow your lens, making it hard to see anything beyond the heaviness. Gratitude gently expands that lens. It doesn't demand that you fake joy or pretend everything's okay. It simply invites you to find *one small thing* that is good. And then another. And another. Over time, those little sparks of acknowledgement, *a warm cup of tea, a sunrise, a kind word, your breath,* begin to reconnect you with life, with hope, with yourself.

Gratitude won't cure anxiety or depression overnight. But practiced consistently, it changes your internal landscape. It builds new emotional habits. It strengthens the neural pathways that say, *"There is beauty here. There is hope here. There is still so much good."*

I've seen this firsthand in my own healing. Gratitude didn't erase the hard stuff, but it gave me the strength to face it with more grace. It gave me permission to expand, to dream, to stretch toward possibility without being paralyzed by guilt or fear. It reminded me that growth doesn't mean rejecting the present; it means building on it with love and self-compassion.

There were seasons when my default setting was lack: not enough health, not enough time, not enough energy, not enough progress, not enough me. And every time I chose to meet that voice with gratitude—real, raw, unfiltered gratitude—I noticed something shift. My breath slowed. My thoughts softened. My belief in myself strengthened.

And the best part? The more I practiced it, the more it became automatic. What used to feel forced eventually became natural, not perfect, but real. Gratitude taught me to see what was already good, to celebrate who I already was. And from there, from that energy, I became someone who could receive more, not from desperation but from wholeness.

I remember a pivotal moment in my early twenties when I was in the depths of my struggle with bulimia, body dysmorphia, and the heavy fog of co-morbid anxiety and depression. I would describe myself as *lost* and *broken.* I was consumed by shame. My relationship with food and my body took up nearly every waking thought, leaving little room for anything else.

I'll never forget what my family doctor, someone I believed could truly see me, beyond the addiction, said to me. In his quiet, grounded wisdom, he suggested that maybe it was okay to accept the eating disorder as part of my life and still move forward. At first, I was confused, even hurt. I took it as him giving up on me, like he didn't believe I could fully heal.

But later, I understood what he truly meant. He wasn't telling me to surrender to the eating disorder. He was reminding me that it didn't *define* me, that I was so much more than what I believed at the time. He was guiding me back to gratitude for the sharpness of my insight, the undeniable light in my beauty, both inside and out, and the fierce, unbreakable drive that refused to be extinguished. With quiet compassion, he was inviting me to see what was already whole and working within me instead of allowing the eating disorder to take the lead role in the story of who I was, to take center stage in my identity.

And that shift, that choice to be grateful for what was *right* with me, even in the middle of my pain? That was a turning point. It helped me build confidence. It gave me a foundation to stand on while I did the challenging, unglamorous work of healing. It reminded me that I didn't need to be "fixed" before I could feel proud of who I already was.

Today, I owe a deep debt of gratitude to that man, my doctor, who never stopped believing I was more than an eating disorder, even during the seasons when I myself doubted that very truth. His belief in me held space for my own belief to grow. This is the kind of gratitude that doesn't gloss over pain. It *holds it gently.* It acknowledges what's hard while still choosing to honor what's strong. It invites you to stop pouring all your energy into what needs fixing and start building from what's whole.

Gratitude isn't just a practice. It's a perspective. It's a way of seeing the world, your life, and yourself through a lens that honors progress over perfection, compassion over criticism, truth over fear.

I practice gratitude the same way I practice mindfulness and awareness, not as something I do once in a while but as a *way of life.* It's a conscious decision, a daily ritual, a non-negotiable. I don't let myself climb out of bed in the morning until I've fully flooded my brain with the feel-good hormones that come from deep, intentional gratitude.

It usually starts simply, with a silent thank you for my warm bed, my pillow, my blankets that wrapped around me like safety through the night. I feel grateful for the roof over my head, for the comfort and beauty that surrounds me, and for the abundance I once only dreamed of. I open my eyes and take it in: the stillness, the softness, the sacred familiarity of home. I feel gratitude for the healing I've done, for the woman I've become, and for the journey that brought me here, even the messy parts. I feel overwhelming gratitude for my sidekick golden retriever, my family, my friends and my work. And yes, by all means, that first cup of coffee deserves a moment of reverence too.

This is how I choose to begin my day, not because life is perfect but because I've learned to *anchor into what's good* before my mind tries to convince me otherwise. Gratitude sets the tone. It shifts my nervous system. It reminds me that I'm already supported, already blessed, already *becoming.* This is gratitude as a lifestyle, as a compass, as a soft place to land and a strong place to rise from.

And when you make it part of your way of being, when it becomes the lens through which you meet the day, everything begins to open. Healing accelerates. Limiting beliefs lose their grip. And your life starts to reflect what you've always secretly known: *there is so much more available to you than fear ever allowed you to believe.*

This is what makes gratitude a superpower in the work of dismantling limiting beliefs. It creates a new internal environment, one where you are no longer surviving on scarcity, but thriving in self-trust. It trains your brain to look for what's possible. It tells your inner child, *"You're safe now."* And it tells your future self, *"I'm already on the way."*

You don't need to be grateful *for* every challenge. But you can always be grateful *within* it—grateful for your strength, for your growth, and for the fact that even on your hardest days, there is something in you still reaching, still rising. And once you start seeing through that lens, everything begins to shift, not all at once, but in the ways that matter most.

I don't just believe this... I live it. And I promise you, this kind of gratitude changes *everything.*

CHAPTER 19

It's Not the End

It's the Becoming

"I'm not who I used to be, and that's the point."

—Unknown

There's a quiet truth about healing and journeying: it doesn't end with the breakthrough. It doesn't end when the tears fall, or when the old belief finally loosens its grip, or even when you feel that beautiful rush of momentum flooding back in. That part—the spark, the shift, the reclaim—is powerful. But it's not the finish line. It's the beginning.

The *real* transformation begins after the book is completed. After the ritual has been done. After life resumes its rhythm and the world asks you, in its own quiet way, **"Will you live this now?"** Because that's the essence of ***becoming***, not just having a powerful moment of clarity, but choosing to honor that moment again and again in the quiet spaces of your everyday life.

The becoming happens in the small, unseen choices, in the way you speak to yourself when no one's listening, in the way you soften when fear rises, and in how you pause instead of spiraling. It's not always big and bold. Sometimes it's whisper-quiet. Sometimes it looks like rest. Sometimes it's just a breath taken with intention, a gentle *no* that protects your peace, or a brave *yes* that expands the vision you have defined.

You're not returning to the old version of yourself; you're *becoming* more *you*, not a shinier, upgraded version built to impress the world but the truest, most grounded, most soul-aligned version you've always been meant to live. And it doesn't require perfection. It asks only for your presence, your honesty, and your willingness to keep coming back to what you know is true, even when it's hard, even when you forget, even when the noise gets loud.

That's what this final chapter is about. It's not the end of your journey. It's the beginning of your ***becoming.*** It's a sacred invitation to keep choosing ***you***, not just when it feels inspiring, but when it matters most. This is the work. This is the walk. This is where the shift becomes who you are.

It's one thing to have an awakening, it's another to *live it.* And that's where so many people get discouraged. They assume the power of transformation lives in the peak moments, the tear-filled breakthroughs, the fire-lit decisions, and the sudden clarity. And yes, those moments matter. They shift something. They open the door. But the real magic? It unfolds in the everyday moments, the steady, soul-led choices to honor your path, again and again, until it becomes who you are.

Insight on its own will move your heart, but it won't rewire your nervous system. That comes through what you *practice*, through what you return to, and through what you embody in the quiet, ordinary moments when no one else is watching. Integration is the process of taking what once felt like a spark and turning it into your steady flame.

It's not glamorous. It's not always inspiring. Sometimes integration looks like brushing your teeth while choosing a better thought. Sometimes it's choosing not to answer that text that pulls you into old energy. Sometimes it's resting when your old self would have pushed. Sometimes it's saying, "*I don't do that anymore,*" not to anyone else, but to yourself.

And here's what's beautiful: the brain doesn't need perfection to rewire. It needs reinforcement, repetition, and compassion. Each time you revisit the truth, each time you remind yourself "*I don't believe that anymore,*" or "*I choose something better,*" you are literally carving new pathways in your brain. It's not just emotional work. It's neurological. It's spiritual. It's real.

And this is why so many people think they've failed when really, they're in the process of *becoming*. They have the insight. They've made the decision. But they haven't yet seen the daily practice for what it is: the place where change *lands*, the sacred space where the mind and body align, where belief becomes biology.

You don't have to feel like your soul is on fire every day. You don't have to get it right every time. You just have to return to the truth, again and again, until the truth becomes your new home. So if you're here, still showing up, even when it's hard, even when it's quiet, please know this: you're not stuck. You're integrating. You're becoming. And that's exactly where the transformation settles in for good.

Recognizing the *Becoming*

Becoming... you recognize it in quiet moments, but don't mistake it for small. It's one of the most powerful shifts you will ever experience, when your inner work begins to take shape in the outside world, when the healing you've done starts speaking through your choices, your presence, your voice.

Becoming is when the version of you that once felt far away begins to rise from within. She's not a vision on the horizon anymore. She's showing up in how you walk, how you speak, and how you say no with grace and yes with boldness. She's in the pause before the reaction, in the moment you soften where you used to shut down, in the boundary you hold without guilt. She's in the breath you take before answering and in the truth you speak without apology. She's *already here*. And that's the ***becoming***.

One of my many ***becoming*** moments stands out vividly. I had long held a vision of becoming a public speaker, not for recognition, but to light something up in people. I wanted to inspire, to awaken, to remind others of what was possible in their own lives. I had asked myself these questions: *What would that version of me look like? How would she lead, speak, and carry herself if she is convinced that she has a gift for getting people excited about their life?*

I had been holding that vision close to my heart for a while when the universe whispered back through a phone call. A representative from our local radio station reached out and asked if I was interested in recording an ad for my practice. I'll never forget his words: *"It's the perfect opportunity to let people know how good you are at what you do."*

In that moment, something inside me stirred with certainty. This was my ***becoming***, not because someone handed me a spotlight but because I recognized it. It was a mirror reflecting back the woman I had already decided to be.

He had spoken the very words I had been declaring to myself day after day while walking into my office, riding that elevator with purpose, breathing through both the nerves and the vision: "I have a gift for inspiring people. I'm good at what I do. The results speak for themselves. I am ready for more." It wasn't coincidence. It was confirmation. It was a powerful reflection of the identity I had been nurturing in silence and was now rising to meet me in the visible world, a reflection of the identity I had anchored into and nurtured long before the world took notice.

And then, as if the universe was responding in kind, everything began to align. Just weeks after that offer, I was invited to be a keynote speaker, an unmistakable confirmation that the inner work was now echoing out into my reality.

Something else was happening… I recognized the voice that rose up instantly, the old story, sharp and familiar, screaming: *Vulnerability! Exposure! Who do you think you are?* I didn't shrink. I didn't silence myself to stay safe. **I chose me. I chose growth. I said yes anyway.** And that changed everything.

I walked into that recording studio, heart pounding, and we recorded the ad. And let me be clear, it wasn't because the fear had disappeared. It hadn't. The ***becoming*** didn't erase the fear. It simply gave me the courage to move with it, beyond it. I remember sitting in my car right before going in, recognizing the tension between the old me and the woman I was stepping into. I felt the pull to play small, to shrink back into safety. But something deeper rose up and said, "*not this time.*" That choice, that breath, that moment of choosing to trust the vision over the fear? That was *powerful.*

And I felt it again—the pride, the alignment, the rising—when I heard that ad play on air the first time, the second time, and the tenth time. With every replay, I reminded myself: "*You did this. You stepped forward. You showed up.*" And dare I say… I knocked it out of the park.

That's what ***becoming*** looks like. That's what it *feels* like.

It's when your old story screams "*Are you crazy?*" And in that moment, you lean into the discomfort because *not* doing it would cost you more than fear ever could. It's when you realize that your future self isn't out there waiting. *She's right here.*

So if you've been wondering whether you're changing, whether this work is "working," whether you're any closer to who you want to be, pause. Look closer. If you're feeling the tension between who you were and who you're becoming, if you're choosing differently, showing up even when it's hard, responding instead of reacting, you're not on the edge of change. You're *in it.* You're ***becoming.***

It may not always feel like a soul-on-fire moment. Sometimes it feels like a single, shaky breath. It's when you realize your transformation isn't coming, it's already unfolding. It's real, and it's yours. You don't need a stage to prove it. You don't need a dramatic breakthrough or a spotlight moment. You just need to keep choosing. Keep showing up. Keep becoming. Because you already are, and it's more powerful than you think.

How to Keep Choosing (Even on Hard Days)

The threat of losing my mother to cancer in 2023 stirred the quiet return of an identity I believed I had long left behind. I found myself buried beneath the familiar weight of an old, worn-out pattern, one that no longer fit who I was but still knew exactly how to pull me back.

And even though I had already done so much work to untangle the limiting beliefs and stories, even though I had walked away from roles that no longer served me, I still felt the old wiring wrap around me like an old, heavy coat I hadn't realized I'd picked back up, not because I wasn't strong but because these roles had once been my way of surviving. And when life got hard, my nervous system defaulted to what it knew best: overfunction, overgive, override.

But this time, I noticed, not because I was fearless but because I was finally listening.

That season asked me to re-choose ***me,*** my life, my path in a deeper, more honest way, not from the peak of a breakthrough but from the heaviness of exhaustion. I had to remember what I already knew. I had to reach back into the truth and bring it forward into the *real world*, into the messy, uncomfortable, demanding parts of life.

And it began, as it often does, with my body. My guidance system, the one I had been ignoring for months in favor of being selfless, being reliable, being everything for everyone was screaming. Fatigue. Irritability. Tightness in my chest. That low, quiet dread in the pit of my stomach. All the signals were there. My body was trying to tell me: *Something is off. Something is misaligned. Something needs your attention.*

I listened. Because one of the most radical things you can do on this journey is trust your inner signals. The tension, the discomfort, the gut knowing these are not signs you're failing. They are invitations. Your body will often tell the truth long before your mind can catch up. And when you learn to respond to that guidance with curiosity instead of judgment, something powerful shifts: you begin to lead yourself back into alignment.

It's not about doing it perfectly. It's about staying present enough to notice when something inside you says, "*this isn't it.*" And then choosing, even with shaking hands, to return to your truth. This transformation is about daily devotion. It's a commitment to the version of you who is rising, not the one shaped by fear but the one anchored in truth, clarity, and worth. It shows up in the small, ordinary moments:

- When you say no without over-explaining.
- When you rest without guilt.
- When you feel the pull to shrink and choose to take up space anyway.
- When you stop waiting for permission and move forward because *you've decided you're ready.*

You keep choosing you by tuning into your body, by trusting your inner signals, and by letting alignment, not fear, lead. You stop asking if you're doing it "right" and start asking, "*Does this feel true? Does this feel like me?*"

There will be days when you forget. There will be moments when the old story feels louder than the new one. But you'll know. You'll feel it in your body. And when you do, you'll return, not with shame but with grace.

And when you do that, when you choose **you,** not just once, but on the hard days, in the hidden moments, and through the tears and the tension, you're not just growing...

You're becoming unshakable.

You Are the Evidence

You don't need someone else to validate your growth. You don't need a certificate, a polished morning routine, or a dramatic breakthrough moment to prove that you've changed. You don't need permission to own the truth: **you are the evidence.**

Every time you've chosen to pause instead of react, you've been doing the work. Every time you took a breath before replying, walked away from something that drained you, or whispered a better belief to yourself in the middle of a hard moment, you were rewriting your story. Every time you honored your boundaries, listened to your body, and said no with clarity or yes with courage, you were *becoming.* It's in the way you return to yourself more quickly now. It's in how you no longer abandon your needs to keep the peace. It's in the way you speak to yourself, with more truth, more tenderness, more respect. It's in the version of you who, even when afraid, still says yes to alignment.

The evidence isn't out there. It's in you. It's in how you walk differently, in how you trust your intuition, and in how you ask better questions, set stronger boundaries, and choose people, places, and practices that reflect your worth. That quiet pull to grow? That rising discomfort in spaces that no longer fit? That wasn't random. That was your becoming calling you forward. And every time you said yes, even when it was messy, even when your voice trembled, you became someone your past self would be so proud of. You may still hear the old voices from time to time. But the fact that you recognize them now? The fact that you don't let them decide who you are anymore? That's everything. That's progress. That's transformation.

So the next time you doubt how far you've come, don't turn away from yourself. Don't minimize the quiet wins or call your growth "no big deal" just because it didn't come with a standing ovation. Stop. Breathe. Let yourself feel the weight of everything you've overcome just to get here. Don't rush past the quiet victories, and don't downplay the work you've done just because it didn't come with applause. Let the truth settle in your bones. You are not who you used to be.

Look in the mirror. Really look. See the strength in your eyes, the steadiness in your breath, the softness you fought so hard to reclaim. See the way you carry yourself now with more clarity, more courage, more truth. You rose. You kept going. You chose yourself when it would've been easier not to. And that matters. It *all* matters.

You are the evidence, the living, breathing proof that transformation is possible and that it's already happening. Right now. In you. It's who you are now. It's in your breath. Your choices. Your boundaries. Your *presence.*

This mindset is no longer just something you practice, it's something you embody. It's the steady, grounded truth that says: "*I know who I am. I know what I deserve. I know where I'm headed."* Because here's what's true: you didn't become someone else through this process. You stripped away everything you weren't. You shed the beliefs, the roles, and the inherited expectations that were never yours to begin with.

And beneath it all, you found her. *You.*

You are not **becoming** someone new. You are **becoming** more *you* than you've ever allowed yourself to be.

So no, this is not the end. This is ignition. This is the threshold of the rest of your life. This is where the insights take root, where the rituals become rhythm, where remembering turns into *knowing.* And you don't need to wait for permission, clarity, or another breakthrough to move forward. You already have everything you need. It's been rising in you all along.

From this moment on, you walk differently. You hold your head higher, not out of arrogance but from truth. You move with conviction. You speak with clarity. You make decisions from alignment, not fear. You keep choosing even when it's hard. You keep choosing, especially when it's quiet. You keep choosing because you've finally remembered what's possible when you do.

This is what it means to live the ***becoming.***

Not perfectly, but powerfully.

Not for show, but for freedom.

Not just in moments, but *as* a movement.

And now? You walk forward, with fire, with faith, and with fierce devotion to your process. You're not behind. You're not broken. You're not late. **You're right on time.**

This is your moment. This is your becoming.

Welcome to your life!

About the Author

Monic Ayotte, Hypnotist and creator of the B.E.C.O.M.I.N.G. Method, is a Registered Psychotherapist and transformational teacher whose work bridges neuroscience, subconscious healing, and soul-aligned growth.

Hailing from the quiet beauty of Northern Ontario, Monic carries her roots with her — grounded, genuine, and full of heart. She blends science and soul in a way that helps people believe in their own transformation again.

Her own journey, one of caregiving, resilience, and learning to rebuild her wellness baseline continues to shape her work and her wisdom. A creative spirit with an ADHD-fueled mind that never stops dreaming, she sees her neurodivergence as her superpower: the spark behind her curiosity, humor, intuition, and endless inspiration.

Though naturally introverted, Monic loves to laugh, share real conversations with her friends and family, and has learned to truly love her own company — those quiet moments where the best ideas are born. She shares her home (and much of her heart) with her golden retriever, Queen Bree, who reminds her daily that joy lives in the simplest moments.

Monic believes, with every part of her, that healing is possible for all of us, that we can design a life by choice, not by default. The only limits that exist are the ones we've agreed to keep.

SCAN HERE FOR
MORE FROM
MONIC AYOTTE

REFERENCES

Beck, A. T. (1976). *Cognitive therapy and the emotional disorders.* International Universities Press.

Bowlby, J. (1988). *A secure base: Parent-child attachment and healthy human development.* Basic Books.

Brown, B. (2010). *The gifts of imperfection.* Hazelden.

Brown, B. (2012). *Daring greatly: How the courage to be vulnerable transforms the way we live, love, parent, and lead.* Gotham Books.

Clear, J. (2018). *Atomic habits: An easy & proven way to build good habits & break bad ones.* Avery.

Dispenza, J. (2012). *Breaking the habit of being yourself: How to lose your mind and create a new one.* Hay House.

Dobson, K. S., & Dozois, D. J. A. (2010). *Handbook of cognitive-behavioral therapies.* Guilford Press.

Doidge, N. (2007). *The brain that changes itself: Stories of personal triumph from the frontiers of brain science.* Penguin.

Dweck, C. S. (2006). *Mindset: The new psychology of success.* Random House.

Hendricks, G. (2009). *The big leap: Conquer your hidden fear and take life to the next level.* HarperOne.

Levine, P. A. (1997). *Waking the tiger: Healing trauma.* North Atlantic Books.Maté, G. (2008). *In the realm of hungry ghosts: Close encounters with addiction.* Knopf Canada.

Maté, G. (2019). *When the body says no: Exploring the stress-disease connection.* Vintage Canada.

Merzenich, M. M. (2013). *Soft-wired: How the new science of brain plasticity can change your life.* Parnassus Publishing.

Porges, S. W. (2011). *The polyvagal theory: Neurophysiological foundations of emotions, attachment, communication, and self-regulation.* W. W. Norton & Company.

Robbins, T. (1991). *Awaken the giant within.* Free Press.

Rohn, J. (n.d.). *Your life does not get better by chance; it gets better by change* [Quote].

Segal, Z. V., Williams, J. M. G., & Teasdale, J. D. (2002). *Mindfulness-based cognitive therapy for depression: A new approach to preventing relapse.* Guilford Press.

Siegel, D. J. (2012). *The developing mind: How relationships and the brain interact to shape who we are.* Guilford Press.

van der Kolk, B. (2014). *The body keeps the score: Brain, mind, and body in the healing of trauma.* Viking.

Made in the USA
Monee, IL
04 November 2026

67374675R00128